UNDERSTANDING CHARLES WRIGHT

Understanding Contemporary American Literature
Matthew J. Bruccoli, Series Editor

Volumes on

Edward Albee • Sherman Alexie • Nicholson Baker • John Barth
Donald Barthelme • The Beats • The Black Mountain Poets
Robert Bly • Raymond Carver • Fred Chappell
Chicano Literature • Contemporary American Drama
Contemporary American Horror Fiction
Contemporary American Literary Theory
Contemporary American Science Fiction, 1926–1970
Contemporary American Science Fiction, 1970–2000
Contemporary Chicana Literature • Robert Coover • James Dickey
E. L. Doctorow • Rita Dove • John Gardner • George Garrett
John Hawkes • Joseph Heller • Lillian Hellman • Beth Henley
John Irving • Randall Jarrell • Charles Johnson • Adrienne Kennedy
William Kennedy • Jack Kerouac • Jamaica Kincaid
Tony Kushner • Ursula K. Le Guin • Denise Levertov
Bernard Malamud • Bobbie Ann Mason • Jill McCorkle
Carson McCullers • W. S. Merwin • Arthur Miller
Toni Morrison's Fiction • Vladimir Nabokov • Gloria Naylor
Joyce Carol Oates • Tim O'Brien • Flannery O'Connor
Cynthia Ozick • Walker Percy • Katherine Anne Porter
Richard Powers • Reynolds Price • Annie Proulx
Thomas Pynchon • Theodore Roethke • Philip Roth
May Sarton • Hubert Selby, Jr. • Mary Lee Settle • Neil Simon
Isaac Bashevis Singer • Jane Smiley • Gary Snyder
William Stafford • Anne Tyler • Kurt Vonnegut
David Foster Wallace • Robert Penn Warren • James Welch
Eudora Welty • Tennessee Williams • August Wilson • Charles Wright

UNDERSTANDING CHARLES WRIGHT

Joe Moffett

The University of South Carolina Press

Published by the University of South Carolina Press
Columbia, South Carolina 29208

www.sc.edu/uscpress

Manufactured in the United States of America

17 16 15 14 13 12 11 10 09 08 10 9 8 7 6 5 4 3 2 1

Library of Congress Cataloging-in-Publication Data

Moffett, Joe.
Understanding Charles Wright / Joe Moffett.
p. cm. — (Understanding contemporary American literature)
Includes bibliographical references and index.
ISBN 978-1-57003-778-8 (alk. paper)
1. Wright, Charles, 1935- —Criticism and interpretation. I. Title.
PS3573.R52Z77 2008
811'.54—dc22

2008030475

Contents

Series Editor's Preface

The volumes of *Understanding Contemporary American Literature* have been planned as guides or companions for students as well as good nonacademic readers. The editor and publisher perceive a need for these volumes because much of the influential contemporary literature makes special demands. Uninitiated readers encounter difficulty in approaching works that depart from the traditional forms and techniques of prose and poetry. Literature relies on conventions, but the conventions keep evolving; new writers form their own conventions—which in time may become familiar. Put simply, *UCAL* provides instruction in how to read certain contemporary writers—identifying and explicating their material, themes, use of language, point of view, structures, symbolism, and responses to experience.

The word *understanding* in the titles was deliberately chosen. Many willing readers lack an adequate understanding of how contemporary literature works; that is, what the author is attempting to express and the means by which it is conveyed. Although the criticism and analysis in the series have been aimed at a level of general accessibility, these introductory volumes are meant to be applied in conjunction with the works they cover. They do not provide a substitute for the works and authors they introduce, but rather prepare the reader for more profitable literary experiences.

M. J. B.

Preface

If international recognition is one measure of a poet's success, then Charles Wright has done well for himself. Wright's poetry has been translated into Spanish, Italian, and French. Starting with his work of the late 1980s, editions of Wright's books have been published in both the United States and the United Kingdom. In 2007 he was awarded both the Italian Leoncino d'Oro award and Canada's Griffin Poetry Award. These accolades are in addition to the critical praise and multitude of awards that Wright has earned in the United States over his four-decade career.

Despite all the attention Wright's work has generated, *Understanding Charles Wright* constitutes the first full-length overview of his poetry. There have been many articles and book reviews on his work, but no monographs that treat the whole of Wright's oeuvre. Adam Giannelli's *High Lonesome* (an update of Tom Andrews' earlier *The Point Where All Things Meet*) collects previously published articles on Wright and reviews of his books. Confined to the latter part of Wright's career, Robert D. Denham's *Charles Wright: A Companion to the Late Poetry* appeared at the very end of my work on this book, and so I could not take full advantage of its resources. *Understanding Charles Wright* represents my contribution to the dialogue that has been conducted on Wright over the last several decades, and it is my hope many more books and essays on him will follow.

I thank the National Humanities Center for providing space and time during a summer seminar for me to work on this book. My gratitude goes to the organizers of the Midwestern Conference on Language, Literature, and Media (MCLLM) for inviting me to share my ideas on Wright in the form of a paper titled "On Mysticism in Charles Wright's *Negative Blue*" at the annual conference held in DeKalb, Illinois, on March 30–31, 2007. There are many individuals for me to thank. Zach Clarke helped with research and editing. Gerry LaFemina offered a fresh perspective as I was completing the book. John Ragsdale, Suzanne Rose, and Tony Lee, my colleagues at Kentucky Wesleyan College, offered various types of support, as did the college library staff who helped me track down some difficult-to-find documents. Robert Denham was more than generous with his insights and research. Of course I must thank Charles Wright himself, who bore my many questions with great patience. Any infelicities that persist are my responsibility.

Thanks go to Kelly and Devon, who provided crucial encouragement. I dedicate my work on this book to Joe, Darla, and Cheyenne Moffett, as well as to the memory of Cheri Okeson.

Abbreviations of Wright's Books

BY	*Buffalo Yoga*
CM	*Country Music*
HL	*Halflife*
NB	*Negative Blue*
QN	*Quarter Notes*
SH	*A Short History of the Shadow*
ST	*Scar Tissue*
TW	*The World of the Ten Thousand Things*

CHAPTER 1

Introduction to Charles Wright

Charles Wright stands among America's most respected contemporary poets. Over the years he has been awarded the Pulitzer Prize, the PEN Translation Prize, the National Book Award, the Lenore Marshall Poetry Prize, the Ruth Lilly Poetry Prize, and a Guggenheim Fellowship, among many other distinctions. From 1999 to 2002 he served as a chancellor of the Academy of American Poets. Wright's critical reputation rests on his engagement with the perennial themes of one's relationship to place and the importance of spirituality in contemporary life. "Language, landscape, and the idea of God" is how he describes the subject of his poems, and his forty-year-long poetic project has been to examine these weighty issues in all their complexity (*QN* 123).

The poet's southern roots play an essential role in his poetry. Wright was born 25 August 1935 in the small town of Pickwick Dam, Tennessee. His mother came from Mississippi, and Wright attributes his pursuit of writing to her. His father was a civil engineer who worked on dam sites, and so the family lived in various locations across the southern states. Most of his early years were spent in Kingsport, Tennessee, a town that figures in many of his poems, including "Two Stories," "A Journal of the Year of the Ox," and "Arrivederci Kingsport."

As a teenager Wright attended Episcopal schools: Sky Valley School when he was fifteen and then Christ School for the last two years of high school; both are in North Carolina. The Episcopal Church had been a presence in his life since childhood, when he served as an acolyte in services. The poet's many poems on the theme of religion testify to the long-lasting effect of his early indoctrination by the church. Wright went on to graduate from Davidson College, also in North Carolina, where he majored in history, in 1957. About Davidson he quipped that it was "four years of amnesia, as much my fault as theirs" (*HL* 60).

After college Wright enlisted in the army. It was during this time, while in Italy, that he began studying poetry after a friend suggested he read Ezra Pound's "'Blandula, Tenulla, Vagula'" and visit the site the poem commemorates. He did so in March 1959 and has declared his "life was changed forever" (*HL* 60). Despite the transformative nature of this experience, it took Wright many years to develop the distinctive poetic voice that he is recognized for today.

Following his time in the army, Wright attended the University of Iowa Writers' Workshop and graduated with an M.F.A. in 1963. He was especially influenced by his teacher Donald Justice, as well as by classmates who would go on to make names for themselves in poetry, such as Mark Strand, and, later, James Tate. Wright has said that during this time his reading included such poets as Wallace Stevens, Robert Lowell, and Philip Larkin (*HL* 172–73).

After returning to Iowa to pursue a Ph.D. in 1965, Wright left a year later to accept teaching work at the University of California, Irvine. He settled in Laguna Beach, a location he says was good for writing because it offered little else for him to do (*HL* 60). Wright also taught and studied in Italy during this period. Italian poets Eugenio Montale and Dino Campana proved important influences on Wright's verse, and he later published well-received translations of both figures.

Wright married Holly McIntire, a photographer, in 1969. The couple has a son, Luke. Holly Wright's photographs often appear on her husband's books, such as on the cover of *Chickamauga,* as well as on the volume of reviews and essays on his work that appeared in 1995, *The Point Where All Things Meet* (revised in 2006 as *High Lonesome*). The importance of the photograph as a tool for memory became a dominant theme of Wright's work in the 1980s.

In 1983 Wright accepted a position at the University of Virginia in Charlottesville, where he currently teaches as Souder Family Professor of English. This move allowed him to return to the South, which has provided the setting of much of his work. Despite his seventeen years in California, Wright's poems are dominated by images drawn from the South and from his time in Italy. When asked about the influence of the Californian landscape, Wright replied, "Never did a thing for me. Never a thing" (*QN* 152). However, some of his poems do take California as their setting, such as "Laguna Blues."

Wright's Project: A Trilogy of Trilogies

With the publication of *Negative Blue* in 2000, Wright completed what has come to be known as his "trilogy of trilogies." The phrase refers to Wright's plan to write three groups of three books of poems each. Thus nine volumes would go into creating this collection of works. After completing each batch of three books, Wright brought them together into a single volume. Not all the poems that appeared in the original, separate books were reprinted in the new "selected" work. *Country Music: Selected Early Poems* (1982) assembles poems from *Hard Freight* (1973), *Bloodlines* (1975), and *China Trace* (1977); *The World of the*

Ten Thousand Things: Poems 1980–1990 (1990) gathers work from *The Southern Cross* (1981), *The Other Side of the River* (1984), and *Zone Journals* (1988); *Negative Blue: Selected Later Poems* (2000) consists of *Chickamauga* (1995), *Black Zodiac* (1997), and *Appalachia* (1998). But these books did not constitute a perfect trilogy of trilogies because with each "selected" volume Wright included other poems. In *Country Music* five poems came from Wright's first book, *The Grave of the Right Hand* (1970); in *The World of the Ten Thousand Things* he included the chapbook *Xionia* (1990); and *Negative Blue* concludes with *North American Bear* (1999). With these additions Wright exceeds his number of nine books, although it could be argued that *Xionia* and *North American Bear* are not books properly speaking, but rather supporting poems respective to each trilogy.

While there may be a mathematical problem with calling this a trilogy of trilogies, the term is useful for describing the structure of the work. It indicates that Wright sees his books relating to one another: the poems are interconnected as themes and motifs reappear over the course of many individual volumes. This is not to say, however, that Wright necessarily had an overarching plan for each part of the project from the beginning. In fact, in an interview with Matthew Cooperman, he admits that *The World of the Ten Thousands Things* was "retroactive structurally" (*QN* 169). It was only after Wright had completed the third volume in that trilogy with its "journal" approach that the earlier books could be appreciated as also being journallike in their form. Thus the structure emerged as the books were completed and was not crystallized before he undertook them.

Allowing a long project to grow organically without a strict sense of structure is not wholly unprecedented in American verse. Charles Olson's *The Maximus Poems* grew over time, with Olson not necessarily intending the work (actually one long poem) to take on the epic proportions that it eventually acquired. The American long poem, a tradition critics see as initiated by Walt Whitman's "Song of Myself," is marked by the poet working on his or her poem for years, often decades, usually with a very loose structure in mind.[1] Whitman's poem itself grew and changed over the several editions the poet produced. A similar situation occurs with such a direct influence on Wright as Ezra Pound whose *Cantos* required decades of work and even then was not completed at the time of the poet's death.

The notion of the trilogy also indicates that Wright sees his work as based on Dante Alighieri's *Divine Comedy*. This epic poem is divided into three sections as its main figure journeys across Hell (*inferno*), through Purgatory (*purgatorio*), and finally ascends to Heaven (*paradiso*), helped along the way by the poet Virgil and Beatrice. Wright points out that his books follow a similar pattern: "In the same way that *Country Music* was a trilogy that was a kind of small-time *inferno, purgatorio,* and *paradiso, Chickamauga, Black Zodiac,* and *Appalachia* are a small-time *inferno, purgatorio,* and *paradiso,*" he relates.[2] The "small time" designation indicates that while Wright may be inspired by Dante, he also realizes he cannot compete with the master. A sense of humility, despite the ambitiousness of a trilogy of trilogies, is an important characteristic of Wright's poetry.

After completing his trilogy of trilogies, Wright published three subsequent books: *A Short History of the Shadow* (2002), *Buffalo Yoga* (2004), and *Scar Tissue* (2006). These books offered a problem for Wright's readers: should his project be regarded as a tetralogy rather than a trilogy?[3] Despite the ambiguity the books presented for some readers, Wright confirms that his trilogy of trilogies does indeed end with *Negative Blue* and does not evolve into a tetralogy of trilogies with the later books.[4] Nevertheless *A Short History of the Shadow, Buffalo Yoga,* and *Scar Tissue* continue with many of the same concerns as those works that came before them, and Wright has indicated there is a correspondence between these three books and the trilogy of trilogies.[5] They also continue with the same style as his previous works, one that has become a recognizable feature of Wright's poetry.

Wright's Style

Wright's poems appearing in the 1970s and thereafter are marked by his use of what has come to be known as a "dropped" line.[6] Here is an example from the poem "After Reading T'ao Ch'ing, I Wander Untethered through the Short Grass":

> I stand inside the word *here*
>   as that word stands in its sentence,
> Unshadowy, half at ease.
>
> Religion's been in a ruin for over a thousand years.
> Why shouldn't the sky be tatters,
>   lost notes to forgotten songs?
>   (*NB* 183)

The phrase, "as that word stands in its sentence" can be understood to be part of the line above it; so too the half-line "lost notes to forgotten songs" belongs to the one preceding it. The dropped line allows the poem to move in increments down the page and plays with the conventional sense of line breaks in poetry. It is a style strongly associated with Wright now, although early in his career his poems carried a more traditional look with lines held tightly against the left margin. Wright explains his breaking of lines this way:

> One of the purposes (one of several) of writing the two-step line I have used on and off since 1978, the low-rider, whatever you want to call it, was to be able to keep the line from breaking under its own weight. In other words, my line began to get longer and more "conversational" as I tried to push it as far toward prose as I thought I could and still maintain it as a verse line. So I began to break the line, in order to keep it whole. It is always one line, not two, and broken in a particular place to keep the integrity of the single line musically. Others who have used the broken line (Pound, Williams, Olson, O'Hara—Justice, even, a few times—and others) used it, for the most part, as two lines (in Williams's case, three lines), as separate entities. Mine is almost always one line, and sounds like one line. To my ear, anyhow. (*QN* 79–80)

Although the dropped lines (or "low-riders") appear to be two separate lines, Wright reveals they are "almost always one line." The technique offers the poet a process by which he can keep related ideas in closer proximity than if they were two separate lines both justified along the left margin of the page. In the present study, following Calvin Bedient's practice, the place where a drop in the line occurs is indicated by a tilde (~) when the poetry is quoted within the body of the text.[7] The dropped line also allows Wright to incorporate the style of his influences into his work. Among the poets Wright mentions here, Ezra Pound is preeminent. Wright's style of lineation is often found by critics and reviewers to be evocative of Pound's, especially that of his *Cantos*.[8]

Wright's poetic line is usually measured by the number of syllables it contains, not where the accents fall, as is typical in poetic meter popular before the twentieth century. When asked why he focuses on an odd number of syllables in his lines, Wright explains, "mostly it was to keep it out of any normal progression, which is to say that if you have even numbers you're more likely to fall into tetrameter or pentameter. Easier to keep it out—but still have the ghost of it—with the odd, because you get an extra little syllable. The seven-syllable line is still my ur-line even now, thirty-five years later."[9] Counting syllables allows him the "ghost" of a form, but using an odd number—seven syllables—helps him avoid falling into a traditional meter such as the eight-syllable line of iambic tetrameter or the ten-syllable line of iambic pentameter. The odd number of syllables permits Wright to forge a distinctive poetic style that both departs from, but also alludes to, past forms.

Aside from literary influences, Wright's poetry is also deeply informed by the work of painters. Critics have shown that the canvases of Paul Cézanne and Giorgio Morandi, the modern Italian artist, influence Wright's poetry. In "Charles Wright, Giorgio Morandi, and the Metaphysics of the Line," Bonnie Costello argues that "in Wright's work the influence of the visual arts carries over from the image to the line. Indeed, in Wright, the line emerges at an alignment of oral and visual impact."[10] In Costello's view the actual look of Wright's poetry, especially his dropped-line poetics, is informed by the visual arts. Cézanne's distinctive way of looking at landscape is particularly important for Wright (*QN* 135). The dropped line Wright employs can be seen as imitating the sense of horizontal rhythm prevalent in paintings by Cézanne. Notably Wright's *Country Music* and *The World of the Ten Thousand Things* use Morandi's and Cézanne's paintings, respectively, as cover art, indicating how closely Wright associates these artists with his own artistic vision.

Two Recurring Themes in Wright's Work: Spirituality and Place

One dominant theme in Wright's work is spirituality. Among Wright's many influences, Gerard Manley Hopkins, the Jesuit poet, occupies a special place.[11] Wright's trip to Hopkins's grave is captured in "Jesuit Graves" in *Black Zodiac,* and the poet uses Hopkins's work as an object of meditation in his journal entry–style essay "Improvisations with Father Hopkins on Lake Como." Hopkins's poems, such as "Carrion Comfort," "Myself Unholy," and "Spring and Fall," with their complicated relationship to God and spirituality, anticipate Wright's similar interest in contemporary spirituality. Wright sees the spiritual quest as an essential element of poetry, as evidenced by his explanation that he considers "the true purpose of poetry to be a contemplation of the divine" (*QN* 120). Given the prevalence of religion in southern culture and Wright's own education at Episcopal schools, it is not surprising that the poet's worldview and his art would be heavily influenced by Christianity. Lee Upton notes that "Wright's is a faith against faith, a resistance to his early indoctrination in the Episcopal Church but not a renunciation of religious strategies for seeking transcendent meaning."[12] This is to say that in Wright's work there is a constant tension between the articles of faith of conventional religion on one hand and a persistent doubt on the other.

At times the doubt appears to border on atheism in Wright's poetry. In "The Silent Generation," for example, one finds, "We walk up and down in the earth, ~ we take our flesh in our teeth. / When we die, we die. The wind blows away our footprints" (*NB*

37). Though the reader does not need to know precisely how Wright feels about religion to come to some conclusion about the poem, it is useful to note that he says in reference to faith, "I think I probably would *like* to believe. I believe in belief, for instance. And it *is* the greatest myth going, isn't it? . . . Just because you don't believe it doesn't mean you don't like to talk about it, or think about it. Besides, I *do* believe in the efficacy of things unseen. It's just that I don't believe in this particular one" (*QN* 119). In its ambiguity this statement, however, does not lay to rest the nature of Wright's faith as he first appears to dismiss conventional religion by calling it a "myth," but then speaks of "the efficacy of things unseen," which seems to gesture toward a mystical perspective on the part of the writer.

As Henry Hart has shown, Wright proves deeply conversant with mysticism.[13] Among his influences are the fourth-century gnostic gospels that were discovered in Egypt in 1945. These texts, known collectively as the Nag Hammadi Library, offer alternative views and teaching of Jesus. In "Watching the Equinox Arrive in Charlottesville, September 1992," for example, Wright paraphrases saying 77 from the Gospel of Thomas: "Jesus said, ~ Lift up the stone and you will find me, / Break open a piece of wood, I'm there. / It's hard to argue with that, / Hard to imagine a paradise beyond what the hand breaks" (*NB* 54). For Wright mysticism is a process of attempting to experience the divine directly, as he identifies in Jesus's suggestion to find the luminous in the everyday things of the world (the stone, the wood). Mysticism is prevalent throughout Wright's work, but it assumes a central position in the poems of *Negative Blue.*

Although Christianity may be Wright's primary point of reference when it comes to spiritual matters, Eastern religion and philosophy play a part as well. In reference to the use of

Christian motifs in his verse, Wright is quick to acknowledge his Eastern leanings: "I would think, as I get older, my steps would be in the service of something more along the line of a Buddhistic journey than a Dantesque journey, as it were," he says (*QN* 124). Again Pound is worth mentioning, this time because of his connection with Eastern culture. Pound's belief in the importance of the image-driven quality of Asian poetry proved a pervasive influence on twentieth-century verse. Wright makes many references in his work to the great Chinese poets Tu Fu and Li Po and to Lao Tzu, the purported writer of the central Chinese Taoist text, *Tao te Ching*.

Wright draws from Asian poetry an engagement with landscape, and often spirituality is linked with place in his poetry, especially in the later books collected in *Negative Blue*.[14] Because of the location of his upbringing and his sense of tradition, Wright's work is steeped in southern culture, particularly that of Appalachia. Adam Giannelli has suggested that Wright's trilogy of trilogies will be titled "The Appalachian Book of the Dead" when published as a whole.[15] This title would tie together all of Wright's work under a designation that specifies the importance of place and metaphysical pursuits in his poetry. "Appalachian Book of the Dead" is a playful variation on the ancient Egyptian Book of the Dead, which carries incantations and offers advice on the afterlife. Appalachia is an area of the country not usually associated with vatic knowledge, and in this way Wright elevates the region to a higher significance.

Although he might imbue landscape with a spiritual power, Wright is also careful to use the term *landscape* and not nature. He argues that "nature is inherently sentimental, landscape is not" (*QN* 85). As an abstraction, landscape offers itself as a tool for Wright's search for the divine, as in his poem "Apologia Pro

Vita Sua," where he declares, "Landscape's a lever of transcendence— ~ jack-wedge it here, / Or here, and step back, / Heave, and a light, a little light, will nimbus your going forth" (*NB* 71). Landscape is directly linked to the divine in "Waiting for Tu Fu": "The landscape, like God, a circle whose center is everywhere / And circumference nowhere" (*NB* 57). In this poem Wright's Eastern and Western influences are mixed, as is often the case in his work. A religiously synthetic vision of landscape is the result in which Eastern and Western philosophies combine to allow the speaker to seek the divine in the world around him.

Wright does not only deal in landscape as an abstraction. His poems are often developed with attention to specific details drawn from his geographical area, such as when he examines his speaker's location in Charlottesville in poems such as "Appalachian Book of the Dead II" and the Blue Ridge Mountains in "Drone and Ostinato." The poet's youth in Tennessee is the subject of "Apologia Pro Vita Sua," as with many other poems. The landscape of Italy also often appears in Wright's work. Geographic details ground Wright's poetry, evoking the places that he loves while providing him sure footing from which to launch into his philosophical meditations.

Wright sees the local as an integral part of poetry; he remarks, "all poetry is local" (*QN* 154). But he also reveals he does not possess one of the stereotypical characteristics of the southerner, the ability to tell great stories: "I can't tell a story. Only Southerner I know who can't. And, in truth, I have no real interest in telling one" (*QN* 107). Wright's confession of his lack of storytelling ability explains why he has not followed other poets and ventured into the realm of fiction. His work is almost exclusively in poetry, although some short nonfiction pieces have appeared over the years and are collected in *Halflife* and *Quarter Notes.*

Ultimately there is no American poet who has combined landscape and spirituality on the scale of Wright. The importance of the local is promoted in long poems by William Carlos Williams in *Paterson* and Charles Olson in *The Maximus Poems,* but these poems are not as spiritually driven as Wright's. Wright's unique gift to the literature of the United States remains his yoking of the everyday in the form of landscape with a conflicted search for spiritual meaning in the world. If James Longenbach is right, that "The Appalachian Book of the Dead" is "sure to be counted among the great long poems of the century," Wright's work will stand with those he admires, especially Pound's *Cantos.*[16]

The discussion that follows covers Wright's "Appalachian Book of the Dead" project along with the development of Wright's early verse style, the shift in Wright's poetry to longer lines, his increased attention to the people and features of the South, and the ongoing search for the divine in Wright's work. The continuities between Wright's earlier work and the three books that follow the trilogy of trilogies—*A Short History of the Shadow, Buffalo Yoga,* and *Scar Tissue*—are also examined. Along the way emphasis is placed on looking at Wright's poems that address the poet's primary concerns of God, language, and landscape.

CHAPTER 2

On *Country Music*

When Wright selected poems for his first trilogy of trilogies, 1982's *Country Music: Selected Early Poems,* he drew on four books: *The Grave of the Right Hand* (1970), *Hard Freight* (1973), *Bloodlines* (1975), and *China Trace* (1977). *Country Music* covers formative years—the decade of the 1970s—in the poet's writing career. Even though the first of these books appeared seven years after Wright had completed his M.F.A. at the University of Iowa, the poems show the poet still growing as an artist and developing his technique. In contrast with Wright's later work, the early poems tend to be abstract and often lack a clear message. As *Country Music* goes on, however, the poems become more direct, filled with references to the southern landscape, and thereby acquire an approach more typical of his subsequent trilogies.

The title *Country Music* alludes to the "white soul" music that influenced Wright (*HL* 53). He describes how he cherished the songs of the early country music group the Carter family in his short essay "A.P. and E.D." Wright compares the songs of A. P. Carter to the poems of one of his main literary influences, Emily Dickinson (*HL* 54). The title *Country Music* also speaks to the rural location of most of Wright's work. Music often is a metaphor poets employ to explain the sonic qualities of their poems, and by emphasizing that his is a "country" music, Wright draws attention to the subject of his poetry. Even when he is writing about faraway locations in Italy, Wright focuses on the landscape or a small village or town; the city almost never figures into his work.

Right after *Country Music* first appeared, it was cowinner of the 1983 National Book Award for Poetry, along with Galway Kinnell's *Selected Poems.* At the time Richard Tillinghast summed up the general critical perspective on the books collected in *County Music:* "This 'country music' is austere and somewhat difficult to access, but its rhythms and images are exquisite and fully reward the reader's effort."[1] In another review from the period of *Country Music*'s first publication, Jay Parini identified a trait in Wright's poetry that became more apparent as time went on: namely that his poems are interconnected. Parini asserted that "individual poems are arresting but none of them quite has its meaning alone. The poems elucidate and comment on each other, extending and developing certain key metaphors and images."[2]

Country Music was reissued in 1991, and Wright wrote in his preface that he remained content with the original selections he had made in 1982. He also endorsed Parini's argument by noting how the various books relate to one another. Wright observes that *The Grave of the Right Hand* works as a "prologue" for the collection, and he continues: "after the prologue, the three following sections (*Hard Freight, Bloodlines,* and *China Trace*) were to represent the present, past, and future" (CM xxiii). *Country Music* constitutes "the first, of a two-part invention" in Wright's plan; the second part would be *The World of the Ten Thousand Things* (CM xxiii). Although at this stage Wright was envisioning his individual books working together to form larger sections in an extended work of two parts, his vision continued to evolve as *Negative Blue* eventually formed a third part and lead to a "trilogy of trilogies."

Among the techniques utilized throughout *Country Music,* the use of second person stands out. The people addressed range widely from Wright's early poetic influence Ezra Pound to his mother and father. This tactic offers the poems a sense of intimacy, as if the reader eavesdrops on conversations the speaker has with his addressees. It also reinforces the general elegiac mood that pervades Wright's early books, especially *Bloodlines,* in which the poet recalls past people and experiences that persist in his memory.

Wright's career-long preoccupation with art begins in *Country Music,* as indicated by the previously mentioned Giorgio Morandi drawing on its cover. Morandi, a favorite artist of Wright's, is known for his work in still life. In a short essay on Morandi, Wright explains that the Italian painter's art "was often thought to be minor, lacking ambition and restricted in scope" (*HL* 7). There is a parallel here in that Wright's poetry has similarly been considered "restricted in scope" by some critics. Calvin Bedient, for example, writes, "Even Sylvia Plath had a bigger tonal range than Wright" because Wright's poems are mostly "melancholy" in nature.[3] The "restricted" tone of Wright's work did not change, however, despite criticisms such as Bedient's. The themes of spirituality and landscape continued to be primary forces in his work, along with the nature of language, from *Country Music* up to *Scar Tissue* (2006).

References to painting techniques populate such poems as "Portrait of the Poet in Abraham von Werdt's Dream," "Northhanger Ridge," "Virgo Descending," "Tattoos," and "Skins" in *Country Music. The World of the Ten Thousand Things* and *Negative Blue* both also include poems that refer to the visual arts, and they likewise bear paintings on their covers that relate to the poetry. *The World of the Ten Thousand Things* utilizes the

Cézanne work and begins with a poem titled "Homage to Paul Cézanne." It closely studies the landscape in a way evocative of the landscape painting on its cover. The front of *Negative Blue* bears a painting by Giovanni di Paolo depicting the expulsion of Adam and Eve from the Garden of Eden. The books completing that trilogy are correspondingly religious in nature. The work of certain painters, especially Morandi, Cézanne, and Mark Rothko, prove influential throughout Wright's career.

The Grave of the Right Hand

Country Music begins with selections from *The Grave of the Right Hand,* but only five poems from this volume make their way into the collection.[4] These poems are distinct from Wright's other work in that they take the form of prose poems. The closest Wright comes to repeating his use of the form is in *Zone Journals* (1988), where the poems appropriate a proselike journal-entry style. The prose poems from *The Grave of the Right Hand* remain unique in Wright's oeuvre in another way: they are closer to little stories than lyric poems, but they do not carry satisfying narratives. Instead these "stories" are as much about their speaker as anything else. "The Voyage," for example, is a poem written in a narratorial voice seemingly drawn from a novel—"For days on end we waited, close by the north-east docks, admiring the stubborn tugs at work"—but the narrative refuses to complete itself (*CM* 5). The poem relates a voyage that failed to happen about which the speaker says, "Eventually, even, some of my friends, sharers of the voyage, vanished. . . ." (*CM* 5; Wright's ellipses).

Lyric poetry is traditionally understood to differ from narrative poetry in that it focuses on the emotional and mental state of the speaker, not story line. Correspondingly the poems of *The*

Grave of the Right Hand are best understood as lyric poems with a veneer of narrative. Wright dismisses *The Grave of the Right Hand* as an "apprentice volume," but its poems anticipate his later writing in the sense that Wright never wavers from his basic lyrical style (*QN* 103). In *The Other Side of the River* (1984) Wright does dabble with narrative on a small scale, but afterward he returns to his nonnarrative, image-based approach. He attributes the lack of narrative in his work to a deficiency in storytelling instinct, but it is also an indication of his lyric sensibility (*QN* 107). Subsequently his trilogy of trilogies is not an epic poem in the manner of canonical texts such as Homer's *Iliad* or Virgil's *Aeneid* that tell stories, but instead is based, as so many twentieth-century long works are, on the lyric. Charles Altieri writes that "the most distinctive feature of the modernist long poem is the desire to achieve epic breadth by relying on structural principles inherent in lyric rather than narrative modes."[5] In his trilogies Wright similarly gestures to epic breadth while using the lyric as his basic building block.

The Grave of the Right Hand introduces not only Wright's dominant mode of the lyric, but also his focus on religion. "Nocturne" contains a reference to a "pilgrim," a figure evoked later in "Skins" in *Bloodlines* (*CM* 6). The location of "Nocturne" is Grotte di Catullo in Sirmione, Italy, the area where Wright first read Pound's "'Blandula, Tenulla, Vagula,'" the poem that inspired Wright's poetry career. About the setting of "Nocturne," the speaker notes, "a strayed traveller, or some misguided pilgrim might, of a summer evening, if he stands quite still and says nothing, imagine he hears the slight off-rhythm of some hexameter line deep in the olive grove, as the slither of night birds moves toward the darker trees. But that is all" (*CM* 6). Although vivid imagistically, the poem is not forthcoming with a message, and if there is a common fault in the prose poems from *The Grave of the Right Hand* that appear in *Country Music,* it is that they all remain vague in their purpose. Yet it is clear that this pilgrim is one who is deeply attentive to the place and its poetry as he hears a "hexameter line" in the grove. With such a reference to Homer, Wright aligns himself with both a great Latin poet (Catullus) and the proverbial source of Greek epic poetry (Homer) while positing himself as a religious seeker (a pilgrim).

Religious imagery is similarly intertwined with a recognition of the importance of place in the first poem in *Country Music,* "Aubade." Wright has said that his work can be read as a "quasi-spiritual autobiography" and this begins with this initial poem of his first trilogy of trilogies.[6] "Aubade" evokes the Mediterranean landscape that appears in "Nocturne" and in many later Wright poems. In "Aubade" the speaker is in Corfu, in Greece, as a note at the end of the poem reveals. The speaker relates, "I, surrendering to the pulse beat of a silence so faint that it seems to come from another country, watch the sun rise over Albania, waiting—calmly, unquestioning—for Saint Spiridion of Holy Memory to arise, leave his silver casket and emerge, wearing the embroidered slippers, from his grove of miracles above the hill" (*CM* 3). Spiridion is the patron saint of potters and of Corfu itself. He is credited with expelling plague from the island and, later, for saving the island from siege by the Turks. Although its setting may be in Europe, the poem shows Wright's linking of religion and place that occurs throughout his work. By the time the reader gets to *Negative Blue,* however, the combination is the American South and mysticism, rather than Greece and conventional Christianity as here.

Hard Freight

Wright's next book, *Hard Freight,* shows him starting to mature as a poet. Toward the end of the book, poems appear that integrate Wright's southern perspective with his general lyrical approach. The poems feel more concrete as a result, with the landscape becoming more vivid in Wright's descriptions. John N. Morris wrote at the time of *Hard Freight*'s publication that "it may be no single poem here has quite the permanent and classic weight" of the title poem of Wright's *The Grave of the Right Hand* (a poem not included in *Country Music*), but Morris noted that he could "everywhere admire the exactness of these verses."[7] Sally M. Gall expressed an opposing point of view by taking Wright to task because "he frantically piles up details, images, similes, and metaphors as if sheer quantity can replace quality of perception. His catalogues can be perniciously boring rather than enlightening."[8] Robert Pinsky was bothered by the abstractions of the book and called it a "frustrating, rich collection."[9] Edward Kessler disparaged Wright's poems because of their lack of clear structure.[10] All this is to say that Wright's early readers generally felt that his poems were not yet living up to their promise but that the poems revealed much potential.

Several poems in *Hard Freight* are homages: to Pound, to the French Symbolist poet Arthur Rimbaud (about whom Wright contends, "Every poet's secret desire is to be Rimbaud" [*HL* 23]), and to Baron Corvo. These poems show the poet self-consciously acknowledging his past influences, but what he is saying about them is not always clear. His "Homage to Ezra Pound," for example, appears as much an invocation of the poet as it is an attempt to say something unique about him. Wright comes closest to making a statement on Pound at the poem's ending, where the speaker expresses hope in seeing Pound regain his greatness. "And you, Pound," the speaker intones,

> Cut loose upon the lagoon (the wind
> Off-shore, and gaining), the tide going out . . .
> Here is your caul and caustic,
> Here is your garment,
> Cold-blooded father of light—
> Rise and be whole again.
>
> (*CM* 12; Wright's ellipses)

The poem takes place in Venice, where Wright, in an interview with J. D. McClatchy, explained he saw Pound in 1969, when Wright was teaching at the University of Padua on a Fulbright. But Wright was hesitant to address the elder poet directly. He recounts, "The closest I ever came was when I stood anonymously next to him under the porticoes of San Marco, looking at the church and piazza one evening. But what was there to say? 'I like your poems.' 'Is this the city of Dioce?' Besides, it was, in the end, the best thing, wasn't it? Standing side by side with him, looking at the most beautiful square in the world, in the city he taught me to look at in ways that would change my life. Water and silence. Some words, I guess, are better left unuttered. Or so they say" (*QN* 97). Given the reverence with which Wright describes Pound here, it is easy to see why the speaker of his "Homage to Ezra Pound" hopes to see the elder poet "rise and be whole again." By this time, Pound's reputation was tarnished. He had been the object of incarceration by U.S. authorities after World War II who sought to put him on trial for treason. The poet had broadcast pro-Fascist diatribes during the war, but ultimately he was found mentally unfit to stand trial in the United

States and returned to Italy. Wright was seeing Pound in those later days of his life, when his best years of writing were behind him. It is little wonder then that the younger poet wanted to see his predecessor restored to his former glory, even if the ending of the poem ("Rise and be whole again") seems more a wish than a realistic possibility.

Several of *Hard Freight*'s homages are directed toward Dino Campana: "Notes for Oscar Wilde at San Miniato," "Oscar Wilde at San Miniato," and "Nocturne" are all noted by Wright to be inspired by the Italian writer. Wright went on to publish a translation of Campana's *Orphic Songs* in 1984. Sections of *Orphic Songs* evoke the mood of the prose poems from *The Grave of the Right Hand* that Wright selected for *Country Music*. However, Wright argues that "there is little about [Campana's] 'lyrics' per se that attract me, and I find there is little to learn from him technically for me at this point. But his spirit has always moved me" (*HL* 123). Nevertheless references to figures as diverse as Pound and Campana show the poet of *Hard Freight* to be quite self-conscious in his relationship to his influences. No other book of Wright's is as directly concerned with past writers as this one. But *Hard Freight* is typical of Wright's poetry in the sense that it reveals his thoughts and current reading interests. Wright is not a poet one has to work hard at to find out what he is thinking about, or reading. The answer is often written right into the poems.

The poet of *Hard Freight* does not only look to literature's past; he also looks to its present. In "The New Poem" Wright explores contemporary poetics. The poem is set up as a series of negatives, a list of what the new poem will not do, and it ends: "It will not attend our sorrow. / It will not console our children. / It will not be able to help us" (*CM* 17). The poem is curious: is

Wright saying that poetry does not have the capability to fix our society—it is unable to "console" or to "help"? This seems an odd possibility, given Wright's status as a poet. Or is Wright identifying what he feels is wrong with current poetic practice? The reader cannot be sure which, if either, of these options is the correct one. Yet it is characteristic of Wright at this stage in his career to leave the reader with ambiguity. In an interview he remarked that this poem is an "antipoem," rooted in the political ferment of the 1960s.[11] Wright says that "everybody was always talking about writing the 'new poem,'" but he decided "there was no new poem that was going to change everything. It would not be able to help us."[12] The poet takes a pragmatic view of literature here, and he admits the poem was a "youthful sort of gesture."[13] Given the high spiritual stakes in Wright's work to come, it is noteworthy that he never again proves quite so dismissive of the power of poetry.

Although Wright might question the social value of literature in *Hard Freight,* this is also the volume in which Wright's distinct lyrical voice begins to emerge in such poems as "White." This poem consists of a series of tercets that are related to one another through their shared images of white:

> The angel, his left hand on your left shoulder;
> The bones, in draped white, at the door;
> The bed-sheets, the pillow-case, your eyes.
>
> *
>
> I write your name for the last time in this mist,
> White breath on the windowpane,
> And watch it vanish. No, it stays there.
>
> (*CM* 21)

Wright's image-driven style, drawn from the poetics of Ezra Pound and William Carlos Williams, is readily visible in the concrete images that appear: the angel, the bones, the bedsheets, the mist, the windowpane all are vividly drawn. These luminous images coalesce in the poem so that the reader is left not so much with a direct statement of the poet's message, but rather an associatively constructed tapestry of haunting imagery.

One of the book's most commonly discussed poems, "Firstborn," movingly tells of the birth of the speaker's son. Wright uses the name of his own son, Luke. Thus the poem begins the mixture of autobiographical and imaginative details that mark Wright's mature work. The poem also shows Wright starting to employ the "dropped" line style of lineation that he utilizes to a greater extent later in his career: "The summer enlarges. ~ You, too, enlarge, / Becoming accessible" (*CM* 23). The poem begins by discussing the child's premature birth, and his arrival recalls the gathering of the Wise Men by the side of Jesus' manger: "We bring what we have to bring; / We give what we have to give; / Welcome, sweet Luke, to your life" (*CM* 22). The allusion to Jesus signifies the miracle of the premature baby's survival and the degree to which he is treasured by his parents, who offer all they "have to give."

The excitement of parenthood aside, the speaker also struggles with the responsibilities of being a new father. Specifically he has trouble deciding what wisdom he will pass on to his son. The speaker asks, "What should one say to a son?" and finally in the fifth section comes to a conclusion (*CM* 24):

> Indenture yourself to the land;
> Imagine you touch its raw edges
> In all weather, time and again;
>
> Imagine its colors; try
> to imitate, day by day,
> The morning's growth and the dusk,

> The movement of all their creatures;
> Surrender yourself, and be glad;
> This is the law that endures.
>
> (*CM* 26)

Wright's advice to connect oneself to the land is not surprising retrospectively, given the intense regionalism of Wright's subsequent work, even that which appears further on in *Country Music.* In the last section of "Firstborn," Wright mentions two of his favorite places: North Carolina and Tennessee. Although Wright's son does not appear in many of his poems, thoughts of him here are combined with references to Wright's beloved southern states and represents a synthesis of what is most dear to the poet in his personal life, as well as his connection with landscape—a combination that becomes an increasingly important characteristic of Wright's verse.

Hard Freight's "Dog Creek Mainline" has been cited by critics and Wright alike as a turning point in his poetic career. Michael Chitwood calls it "the poem where Wright began focusing at least as much on content as technical matters."[14] The first stanza reads:

> Dog Creek: cat track and bird splay,
> Spindrift and windfall; woodrot;
> Odor of muscadine, the blue creep
> Of kingsnake and copperhead;
> Nightweed; frog spit and floating heart,
> Backwash and snag pool: Dog Creek.
>
> (*CM* 36)

And the list continues. The particulars of the flora and fauna from Wright's early life in the South come through: the muscadine, the copperhead. Wright says of this piece: "From the poem

'Dog Creek Mainline' on, I've been very conscious of content. Before that, in *The Grave of the Right Hand* and the first third of *Hard Freight,* I was much more interested in just putting the poem together. Now I'm interested in putting it together the best and most interesting way I can and also saying whatever it is I have to say" (*HL* 86).

"Dog Creek Mainline" ends with Wright noting,

> The heart is a hieroglyph;
> The fingers, like praying mantises, poise
> Over what they have once loved;
> The ear, cold cave, is an absence,
> Tapping its own thin wires;
> The eye turns in on itself.
>
> (*CM* 37)

Wright has shifted in perspective at the end of the poem from the distinct features of the landscape to the features of the speaker himself, an individual who looks inward ("the eye turns in on itself") to find what he values, what is in his "heart." Part of what is in his heart is of course the elements of the landscape that he has named at the beginning of the poem.

Other poems in *Hard Freight* carry specific references to the speaker's youth in the South, "Blackwater Mountain" and "Sky Valley Rider" in particular. "Blackwater Mountain" again uses scenes of nature and recounts a hunting trip during which the speaker, as an adolescent, waited for an unnamed adult, "for two hours, waist-deep in the lake, / The thicket as black as death, / Without success or reprieve" (*CM* 38). This speaker is now himself an adult and instead of a gun carries a flashlight that he shines into the dark: "I stand where we stood before and aim / My flashlight down to the lake. A black duck / Explodes to my right, hangs, and is gone. / He shows me the way to you" (*CM* 38). The poem mixes memory and regret as the speaker thinks back to his youth and yearns for the missing person. "Sky Valley Rider" is similar in that it too communicates a mood of melancholy as it describes "two thousand acres of loneliness" while "the past, wrecked accordion, plays on, its one tune / My song" (*CM* 40). Sky Valley School was one of Wright's places of education, and the speaker of the poem has trouble reconciling his memories of the past in any sort of happy way.

The final poem of *Hard Freight*, "Clinchfield Station," contains some of the book's finest lyricism. In the second part of the poem, Wright asks,

> Father advise us, sift our sins—
> Ferry us back and step down;
> Dock at the Clinchfield Station:
>
> Our Lady of Knoxville reclines there
> On her hard bed; a golf club
> Hums in the grass. The days, dry cat tracks, come round,
> A silence beneath the leaves:
>
> The way back is always into the earth.
>
> (*CM* 48)

Wright's combination of the local (Clinchfield Station and Knoxville, Tennessee) and the universal (our sins) proves a distinctive feature of his work. In this poem even an everyday item as simple as a golf club takes on a life of its own and "hums in the grass." "The way back" is presumably back to where we were before we were born on this earth, and Wright says only through death can we find our way to that origin. Religious overtones also appear in "Northhanger Ridge" and "Primogeniture" in *Hard Freight.* With its focus on the divine and the local, memory and melancholy, the volume anticipates the work that appears in Wright's next book, *Bloodlines.*

Bloodlines

David St. John suggests that *Bloodlines* is a "fiercely elegiac book" in that it expresses a pervading sense of loss (*CM* xv). The book was selected for the Academy of American Poets' Edgar Allan Poe Award. Peter Stitt writes that "*Bloodlines* is a book in which Charles Wright goes back to his origins—into family history, personal history, even into the history of the region of the country in which he grew up," but Stitt argues that "the poems in *Bloodlines,* however, are curiously bloodless."[15] Part of the problem with the many abstractions in Wright's early poems is that people figure little in the work, making the poems "bloodless" in Stitt's words. Wright attempts to remedy this deficiency in *The World of the Ten Thousand Things,* but it is an ongoing concern for some readers of Wright's verse. Stitt's criticism could also be leveled, for example, at the poems of *Negative Blue* since landscape is discussed far more frequently there than any of the people who inhabit it.

In a review John N. Morris argued that "*Bloodlines* is not quite so sustained a performance as *Hard Freight,*" although he also noted that "in *Bloodlines,* to be sure, much is much the same."[16] Morris also complained that sometimes Wright's "devices leave us a little too much to our own."[17] Wright's strategy of writing in such a way that the reader is left with ambiguity and must play a pivotal role in deriving meaning from the poems is clearly problematic for Morris. On the other hand, Carol Muske identified in Wright's verse during this period "a fullblown and recognizable style."[18] In many places in his work

Wright acknowledges the importance of style, claiming that "style is everything and nothing at the same time. But mostly it is everything" (*HL* 36).

Among the selections of *Bloodlines,* those most frequently discussed by critics are "Tattoos" and "Skins." These multipart poems anticipate the book-length sequence of Wright's next volume, *China Trace.* They take the form of twenty sonnetlike sections, but Helen Vendler points out, "Though these have of course affinities with sonnets, they are sonnets that go nowhere, or end where they began: either the second half of the poem repeats the first, or the last line reenters the universe where the first line left it."[19] Vendler identifies here one of the concerns readers have with Wright's early poems: that they are elliptical or obscure and the poems do not necessarily arrive at a conclusion. This is a particular problem with "Skins" and "Tattoos," since the sonnet form demands closure. In the traditional Shakespearean sonnet the last two lines provide a summarizing message for the poem. By contrast, in "Tattoos" and "Skins," Wright cultivates a poetics of incompleteness that often leaves his reader expecting more that fails to come.

The poet describes the content of "Tattoos" as "psychic tattoo[s]"—they are experiences that occurred in his life, emphasized by the dates supplied at the bottom of each section that correspond to years the events occurred (*HL* 67). As Peter Stitt argues, it would be quite difficult for the reader to gather what is going on in each section without the helpful notes that Wright added when "Tattoos" was reprinted in *Country Music.*[20] Wright's decision to add short explanations is evocative of T.S. Eliot's addition of notes to his famous modernist long poem "The Waste Land" after the fact. As with Eliot's endnotes, Wright's help to clarify the action of the poems.

"Tattoos" puts more of the poet's life into his work than the reader has encountered previously. The speaker tells of his early years, especially his experience as an acolyte in church in section 5 of the poem. Section 5 recounts an episode of Wright's fainting at the altar, brought about by the Episcopal practice of fasting before receiving the Eucharist (*HL* 74). Other moments of the speaker's childhood include attending writing class, where he describes in section 12, "The words, like bees in a sweet ink, cluster and drone" (*CM* 67). Section 13 relates what appears to be a case of sexual abuse of the speaker by the janitor at his school. A note names the location in this section as Corinth, Mississippi—one of Wright's boyhood homes.

The deaths of Wright's father and mother figure largely in "Tattoos." The passing of Wright's mother is memorialized in section 15. His father is evoked in section 2 by a favorite phrase of his, "*duck soup*" (*CM* 57), which Wright says means something is "incredibly simple" (*HL* 70). The death of the father is remembered obliquely in section 19: "*The left shoe. / The left glove. / Someone is dead; someone who loved them is dead*" (*CM* 74). But for all his sense of loss, the speaker decides, "Regret is what anchors me" (*CM* 74). The speaker finds serenity in death, despite the difficulty of his loss, and the challenge of reconciling one's self to the mystery of death recurs in many later poems.

The speaker's psyche is a subject of the sequence as well. Dreams form the basis of sections 14 and 17. An awareness of the speaker's own mortality is revealed in a car accident recounted in section 11. Wright speaks of "black stretcher straps," the "click of a scalpel; glass shards / Eased one by one from the flesh" (*CM* 66). He asks, "what do we do with this, / Rechuted, reworked into our same lives, no one / To answer to," and he concludes, "We stand fast, friend, we stand fast" (*CM* 66). The ambiguity of many of Wright's early poems is not present here; in these lines he directly addresses the importance of facing one's problems—"standing fast," he says—as he considers where his life will lead him after the accident.

The focus on the physical body that emerges in section 11 is echoed elsewhere in the sequence. Section 7 is an ekphrastic poem of *The Resurrection* by Piero della Francesca.[21] Wright focuses on the features of Jesus's resurrected body: "His eyes twin lenses, and ready to unroll. // Arm and a leg, nail hole and knucklebone, / He stands up" (*CM* 62). The image of the wounded body of the savior is offset by the sexuality of the body in section 16, where a sideshow stripper is described as "all gloss, gothic and garrulous, staked / To her own tree, she takes it off, / Half-dollar an article" (*CM* 71). A preoccupation with corporeality also appears in section 8, this time Wright describing a man identified as Harold Schimmel who performs his morning prayers: "His nude body waist deep in the waves, / The book a fire in his hands" (*CM* 63). It was Schimmel who suggested Wright read Pound's poem in Italy that inspired his poetry career (*HL* 149). These contrasting images of the body represent the different sides of Wright's poetics: the divine and the profane. They also reveal the intensely observed details of the everyday that mark his work. As the poet himself points out, his poems do not begin in his imagination, but rather in what he has observed (*QN* 108).

Wright admits that "Skins" is even more abstract than "Tattoos." The poet explains, "I knew that later I would write something that would be conceptual, that I was going to play off the conceptual and theoretical poem against 'Tattoos'" (*HL* 67). He continues, noting that "'Skins' is about such things as truth, beauty, the eventual destruction of the universe, metamorphosis, that kind of thing. They are supposed to be abstract and musical against the actual" (*HL* 67). As with "Tattoos," there are twenty sections, and the poems each contain fourteen lines. Notes are again employed, but these notes are so vague, using one- or two-word descriptions such as "Truth," "Water," or "Earth/Fire," that the reader is helped little by them (*CM* 102).

Section 1 of "Skins" declares, "There comes that moment / When what you are is what you will be / Until the end, no matter / What prayer you answer to" (*CM* 82). The sense of inevitability that emerges in these lines sets up the idea that what follows in the poem is also inevitable, just as the events of the speaker's life in "Tattoos" lead him to become the person he is. Section 1 thus argues for viewing inescapable forces that come to dictate our lives, much in the same way Wright's upbringing in the South makes him the person, and poet, he is.

"Skins" proves a meditation on a perennial theme of Wright's —the divine—but other abstractions, such as beauty, also receive attention. In fact, a focus on beauty occurs in section 2. This section foregrounds art's ability to produce aesthetic pleasure in the viewer by referring to a religious painting, emphasizing, "the brushstroke that holds the angel's wing / Back from perfection" (*CM* 83). Wright then reveals, "In all beauty there lies / Something inhuman, something you can't know" (*CM* 83). The line break on *lies* suggests that beauty lies; that is, beauty is not something humanity can count on for always telling the truth—it is deceptive. It is also unknowable and somehow "inhuman," the speaker says.

Even for all the abstractions in "Skins," Wright grounds the poem by talking of the very earth itself. Section 9 states:

The earth is what salivates, what sticks like a new glue.
It is to walk on, it is to lie down in,
A sure sheet for the resurrection.
The earth is what follows you,
Tracing your footsteps, counting your teeth, father
And son, father and grandson.

(*CM* 90)

Wright ultimately shows that the earth promises release: "Your socks sink in the dirt, all pain gone" (*CM* 90). In a book so filled with death, this passage provides a healing image in which the pain that humans may feel while "walking" or "lying" on the earth is also promised to pass away eventually when we die and become part of the earth again.

The religious motif of "Skins" remains consistent to the end. Section 19 says, "You thought you climbed, and all the while you descended / Go up and go down; what other work is there / For you to do, what other work in this world?" (*CM* 100). The rhetorical question becomes a strategy Wright uses while meditating on religious themes. In section 20 the poet significantly calls his protagonist a "pilgrim" and revisits the motif of the journey from section 19:

And what does it come to, Pilgrim,
This walking to and fro on the earth, knowing
That nothing changes, or everything;
And only, to tell it, these sad marks,
Phrases half-parsed, ellipses and scratches across the dirt?
It comes to a point. It comes and it goes.

(*CM* 101)

The poem ends here without providing a definitive answer to Wright's question of what it all "comes to." But by virtue of the fact that the character is a pilgrim, it can be understood that he will continue on his religious search and the destination itself will be death and after that, he hopes, unification with the divine. The pilgrim's "walking to and fro on the earth" is not necessarily an activity to be lamented but rather part of the inevitability of his existence while alive.

Near the end of *Bloodlines,* Wright returns once more to the issue of his parents' deaths. His father's passing is recounted in "Hardin County" and his mother's in "Delta Traveller." Wright explains about his mother in an interview: "I facetiously said once that I write for my mother, and in fact I do write for her because she always wanted me to be a writer. There are very few mothers who want their children to be writers and she desperately wanted me to" (*HL* 128). In "Delta Traveller" the speaker appears to reconcile himself to death and surprisingly finds that

> the dead are brought
> Back to us, piece by piece—
> Under the sponged log, inside the stump,
> They shine with their secret lives, and grow
> Big with their messages, wings
> Beginning to stir, paths fixed and hearts clocked,
> Rising and falling back and rising.
>
> (*CM* 81)

The speaker finishes the poem with a redeeming thought: that the dead return, buoyed by wings like those of angels. Death is not a punishment, but rather a release in which we become more than what we were when alive.

Bloodlines continues its elegiac mood up to the final poems of the book. In "Link Chain" the speaker observes, "Each tree I look at contains my coffin," and in "Bays Mountain Covenant" he says he speaks "for my own death and the deaths that will follow me" (*CM* 104, 106). "Rural Route," though it starts with an image of the dead—"The stars come out to graze, wild-eyed in the new dark. / The dead squeeze close together"—ends with an image of the speaker's life: "I am back on the West Coast, in my studio, / My wife and my son asleep" (*CM* 107, 108). In the three-part structure of this first trilogy, *Hard Freight* represents the present, *Bloodlines* the past, and *China Trace* the future. With its intense focus on death, it is easy to see how *Bloodlines* fits this scheme: it is a book that is steeped in the lived past of its speaker. *China Trace* on the other hand does indeed look to the future, although it proves one that also leads to its speaker's eventual departure from the earth.

China Trace

Wright confesses to Sherod Santos that he thought *China Trace* would be a major book for him, but he was disappointed by the reception it received from readers (*HL* 99–100). With the book he experienced a "feeling that I'd done it, I'd really written the book I had wanted to write" (*HL* 99). In a review from the time, Joseph Garrison agreed with Wright and said he saw it as "Wright's best and most accessible book to date."[22] But other reviewers, such as Peter Stitt, who has long been one of Wright's frankest critics, felt lost in the abstractions of the book. "Lyricism is still present in *China Trace,*" he wrote, "but the clarity is long since gone, having been finally put to rest in *Bloodlines.*"[23] Richard Jackson similarly noted that the poems of *China Trace* are often "inexcusably vague, or inaccessibly solipsistic."[24] However, even fifteen years after its publication, Wright admitted it was still one of his favorite books (*QN* 133). The poet reveals that the structure of the trilogy, and thus where he goes with *China Trace,* became clear to him relatively early on: "A third of the way through *Hard Freight* I could see to the end of *China Trace*" (*HL* 138).

The title of the book is influenced by Wright's mother's place of derivation: "my mother was from Mississippi and I have always loved the phrase *Natchez Trace.* It has a wonderful sound. Trace being a road to somewhere, of course. So this would be the China trace, the attempt to follow the road to a Chinese resolution of certain emotional aspirations" (*HL* 133). *China Trace* can be distinguished from the books that come before it in many ways. Perhaps most important is that this collection is conceived as a book-length sequence by Wright. The poet explains the format thus: "The 'character' going from religious release (childhood) through an attempted ascension, ends up stuck in the Heaven of the Fixed Stars (in the Dantescan cosmology), a man-made heaven. Divine guidance and intervention is missing. It is a willed assumption, and he can go no higher as he only believes what he can see. But there he is, after forty-six chapters in his own book-length poem, pasted onto the sky, a day late and dollar short" (*HL* 29–30). Though Wright mentions forty-six chapters, when the book was originally published, it carried fifty—four were eliminated as he made selections for *Country Music.* Early on he describes these fifty sections as "fifty little doors you open, click shut, and then go on to the next" (*HL* 97). Wright's description of the general narrative arc of the sequence, that it starts in the speaker's childhood and ends in his ascension to the stars, makes the book sound far more narratively driven than it really is. If anything, the sections explore the emotional and spiritual states of the speaker but carry very little action.

The "little doors" that Wright describes lead the reader to many different rooms. Several of them, curiously enough, are occupied by dogs. Michael Chitwood observes that dogs appear often in Wright's work, and that is certainly the case here.[25] Dogs are present in "Childhood," "Dog," "Wishes," and "Dino Campana," and phrases with "dog" in them appear as well: "dogwood," "hangdog," and "dog rose" (*CM* 144, 146, 148). One poem is titled "Captain Dog," which Wright clarifies is a nickname his students once had for him (*HL* 81). Of the significance of dogs, he playfully points out that "there is also the reverse spelling of dog," which of course is "god" (*HL* 81). If the reader imagines every time he or she reads the word "dog" that "god" is encoded in it, then the divine is an even larger presence in *China Trace* than that observable at first glance. The dog might be seen to represent Wright's investment in the mundane. In *Halflife,* Wright speaks of "the metaphysics of the quotidian, the metaphysics of the everyday" that underlies his work (*HL* 97). In this way the dog can be viewed as an expression of the "quotidian" at the same time it gestures to the divine, the "metaphysical" in everyday life.

Religion and religious reveries are nothing new to Wright's work at this point in his career, but what is different in *China Trace* is the directness with which Wright speaks about God. God does not always appear a positive force, however. In "Invisible Landscape," Wright argues, "God is the sleight-of-hand in the fireweed, the lost / Moment that stopped to grieve and moved on" (*CM* 134). In "Thinking of Georg Trakl," the reader finds, "Finger by finger, above Orion, God's blue hand unfolds" (*CM* 149). The focus on "blue" anticipates the title of the third trilogy, *Negative Blue.* "Clear Night" finds the speaker directly stating his desire to commune with his creator:

I want to be bruised by God
I want to be strung up in a strong light and singled out.

I want to be stretched, like music wrung from a dropped seed.
I want to be entered and picked clean.

(*CM* 152)

The speaker wants God to be proved to him empirically. David St. John suggests that "*China Trace* is a pilgrim's book, the same 'Pilgrim' who is addressed at the conclusion of 'Skins'" (*CM* xvii). If this assertion is true, then it is a quite different kind of pilgrim in Wright's poem from the conventional notion of a pilgrim as a devoted religious follower.

In fact, this pilgrim is often at a loss in the world. The speaker notes in "1975" that "At 40, the apricot / Seems raised to a higher power, the fire ant and the weed. / And I turn in the wind, / Not knowing what sign to make, or where I should kneel" (*CM* 125). Although he is lost, the speaker still wishes to express his respect by making a sign or kneeling. A related poem, in terms of the confusion of the speaker, is "Stone Canyon Nocturne." Of this poem, Wright says that it is "a central poem in the book" and "the poem contains things that I believe very deeply" (*HL* 83). At "Stone Canyon Nocturne's" conclusion, the reader finds, "Like a bead of clear oil the Healer revolves through the night wind, / Part eye, part tear, unwilling to recognize us" (*CM* 139). If the "Healer" is God—and there is no reason to believe otherwise—then the speaker expresses a profound bewilderment, almost an anger, at God for his reticence. The Healer is figured as an eye, a tear, and in this metaphor the emotion of the speaker is expressed: he weeps for the lack of acknowledgment by his Creator.

As occurs throughout Wright's work, the conflict the speaker feels about Western religion is eased by a turn to Eastern philosophy. The quote credited to T'u Lung that ends the book provides resolution for the speaker: "I would like to house my spirit within my body. . . . And so, being unable to find peace within myself, I made use of the external surroundings to calm my spirit, and being unable to find delight within my heart, I borrowed a landscape to please it" (*CM* 157). These lines highlight again the importance of landscape for Wright and explain some of the peace his speaker seeks in it. An engagement with Asian themes is also evident in the book in the concept of the Chinese ideogram that informs the title of one poem, "Spider Crystal Ascension." The ideogram had fascinated Ezra Pound as he understood it through the work of Ernest Fenollosa. For Pound the ideogram was both word and image and thus united his love for language and for visual representation. He uses ideograms often in *The Cantos*. Wright admits to knowing "nothing" about Chinese ideograms but also concedes, "I agree with Pound: it must be a wonderful way to write, to be able to see, physically, what you're saying" and he goes on to relate that in "Spider Crystal Ascension," "The title is three separate words that are supposed to give you an idea of what's coming in the whole poem" (*HL* 79). The words thereby attempt to work ideogrammatically, seeking to produce image associations in the mind of the reader.

Art itself becomes a solace, almost a kind of religious vocation, in *China Trace*. In "Reunion"—a poem Wright anticipated many readers would find objectionable (*HL* 82)—he announces: "I write poems to untie myself, to do penance and disappear / Through the upper right-hand corner of things, to say grace" (*CM* 141). Elsewhere he says, "Poems are sacred texts" (*HL* 129). The poem thus allows the speaker to express his desire for religiosity, as well as to overcome himself—to "untie myself," he contends. Wright's ongoing passion for painting is expressed in these poems as well, with his favorite painters, such as Morandi and Edvard Munch, making appearances within poems or announced in titles. Whether it is a poem or a painting, the speaker seeks the divine in art, much in the same way he seeks it in the natural world around him.

In the final section of the sequence, "Him," Wright reveals the fate of his pilgrim: "His sorrow hangs like a heart in the star-flowered boundary tree. / It mirrors the endless wind," and the reader is instructed to "look for him high in the flat black of the northern Pacific sky, / Released in his suit of lights, ~ lifted and laid clear" (*CM* 156). The pilgrim has now made his ascension as he has gone up to be part of the stars. But, as Wright says, it is "a man-made heaven. Divine guidance and intervention is missing." The "bruise" from God that the speaker needed did not appear. His lack of faith has left him alone, hanging among the stars but not ascended to what he had hoped would be his final heavenly destination.

Despite the rather somber ending of the sequence, *China Trace* also introduces an element of playfulness, particularly wordplay, to Wright's work that was rarely evident before. This playfulness appears in the god/dog pun, and it is observable in the title of the last section of *China Trace*. The poet says, "'Hymn' is the other point of the title 'Him,' of course" (*HL* 130). The main character of the poem becomes his own religious song, his own "hymn." Wright thus maintains a certain ironic distance from the speaker of *China Trace*. But the humor in Wright's work at this stage is clear only when the poet explains his poems; there is little on their surface to suggest more light-hearted intentions. In fact, their tone, as evident in the extracts examined here, is quite serious. The situation is different by the time Wright composes *Negative Blue,* which carries many ironic titles and humor embedded within the poems themselves.

Certain elements of Wright's poetic style begin to solidify in *China Trace*. "California Twilight" begins, "Late evening, July, and no one at home. / In the green lungs of the willow, fly-worms and lightning bugs / Blood-spot the whips and wings" (*CM* 130). In *Negative Blue* many of Wright's poems begin in exactly this manner, by establishing the location of the poem, and often the season of the year in which it occurs, before the speaker elaborates on an insight he has or a philosophical or religious meditation he wishes to impart. In "California Twilight" the speaker goes on to ask, "What was it I had in mind?" as he hears a skateboard go down the street (*CM* 130). In Wright's later verse, the speaker similarly sits and contemplates as the world goes on around him. "California Twilight" ends with arresting, surreal imagery: "Slowly the furred hands of the dead flutter up from their caves, / A little pinkish flame is snuffed in my mouth" (*CM* 130). Although it takes some imagination on the reader's part to picture what a pink flame would look like in a person's mouth, the image is effective in expressing the otherworldly sensation the poet experiences when he considers everyday things such as lightning bugs and skateboards. Compare this imagery with the following from *Negative Blue:* "We walk up and down in the earth, ~ we take our flesh in our teeth" (*NB* 37). How exactly "we" can "take our flesh in our teeth" is challenging to imagine, but intuitively the image makes sense. The poem is operating on the level of association, not logic, and this approach continues to be prevalent in Wright's later work. The poet says he is "an emotional person, more often than I am a reasoning person,"[26] and these images are correspondingly based more on emotional rather than logical responses to the world.[27]

When *China Trace* was originally published, it carried a blurb on the book's back cover that described it as the end of a trilogy.

Peter Stitt responded by saying, "I confess to having only the vaguest notion of why they might constitute a trilogy; the conceptual basis of these books is too private, at least for now."[28] Looking back at his first trilogy, Wright comments, "this is the book I was trying to write all those years, *Country Music.* For fifteen years, I was trying to write this book, and it wasn't until I got started on *Hard Freight* that I really saw the scope of what I wanted. . . . I was asked to do a Selected Poems and I said, only if I can do the poems—those four books—from Wesleyan, no new things. I wanted a chance to get this together as a unit" (*HL* 138). Although readers such as Stitt failed to appreciate the contour of Wright's first trilogy at the time of its completion, clearly the poet saw it relatively early on. Retrospectively the reader finds that many of Wright's themes—religion, self, art—begin to take shape there, as does his poetic style. His next trilogy, *The World of the Ten Thousand Things,* only further develops the aesthetic vision that finds its origin in *Country Music.*

CHAPTER 3

On *The World of the Ten Thousand Things*

The World of the Ten Thousand Things: Poems 1980–1990 contains selections from *The Southern Cross* (1981), *The Other Side of the River* (1984), *Zone Journals* (1988), and *Xionia* (1990). With the publication of this collection, many readers viewed Wright as entering a mature phase of his work. J. D. McClatchy wrote in a review, "There is no book published this year I could recommend more highly."[1] He pointed especially to the success of *The Southern Cross,* about which another reviewer had said, "[the book] is the work of a master writing at the height of his powers, and signals a number of directions that I'd guess some of the best poetry of the eighties will follow."[2] Although his influence on poetry of the decade is debatable, Wright's importance was being recognized. He was nominated for the National Book Critics Circle Award for *The Other Side of the River* in 1984, and he received the Brandeis Creative Arts Citation for Poetry in 1987.

The themes of *The World of the Ten Thousand Things* include geography, a continuing concern for the poet. It was during this period, in 1983, that Wright moved to Virginia after seventeen years of living in California. Although California figures into the poems more than before, the poet admits, "I have no emotional stake in California" (*HL* 159). Perhaps this is why the poems are more restless, geographically, than those that came previously. Often within the course of a single piece a number of locations from the poet's past may be mentioned, such as the title poem of *The Southern Cross* that shifts between Tennessee, Montana, and Italy. The places themselves are depicted in greater detail, and Wright's examination of his relationship to landscape continues. Yet, while landscape continues to dominate thematically in *The World of the Ten Thousand Things,* this part of the trilogy of trilogies contains the most people, especially in *The Other Side of the River.* Wright's representation of people complements his descriptions of landscape and ultimately emphasizes the connection between person and place.

Painting proves another prominent theme, with Paul Cézanne's *Bend in the Road* on the cover of the book. Wright states that the technique of painters such as Cézanne appeals to him as a poet: "I like layers of paint on the canvas. I also know after I'm tired of lots of layers on the canvas, I'm going to want just one layer of paint and some of the canvas showing through" (*HL* 66). The canvas does peek through in Cézanne's painting, and Wright similarly strives to exploit white space between stanzas on the page (*HL* 85). He writes of a strategy of "using stanzas in the way a painter will build up blocks of color, each disparate and often discrete, to make an overall representation that, taken in its pieces and slashes and dabs seems to have no coherence, but seen in its totality, when it's finished, turns out to be very recognizable landscape, or whatever. Cézanne is someone who does this, in his later work, to an almost magical perfection. I'd like to be able to write poems the way he painted pictures" (*HL* 85). In "Halflife: A Commonplace Notebook," Wright again discusses Cézanne's importance. He says he seeks to use "tonal blocks, in tonal units that work off one another," and then he suggests to the reader, "Vide Cézanne's use of color and form" (*HL* 20). The result is that Wright's poems often carry the postimpressionistic style of artists such as Cézanne, as opposed to a realist approach that seeks to represent the world in all its fine, and sometimes gritty, reality. Instead works such as Cézanne's offer an atmospheric approach while rendering their subject in a very self-reflexive way with the foregrounding of technique. Wright's work is similarly marked by a heavy stylization.

The poet's verse style continues to evolve in this trilogy as his poems grow longer and longer, both in terms of stanzaic number and line length. He admits that "one of my prime interests in lengthening my own line was to see just how long I could make it and still have it be an imagistically oriented line and not a discursive, or narrative-based line: the extended, image-freighted line that doesn't implode or break under its own weight" (*HL* 183). Wright thus stays true to the imagistic poetics he inherits from Ezra Pound and Emily Dickinson while looking more and more on the page like that other great American nineteenth-century poet, aside from Dickinson: Walt Whitman. In fact, Whitman's influence on Wright's work has been noted by J. D. McClatchy, who says of the trilogy of trilogies, "what I read is a twentieth-century *Song of Myself*."[3]

Other influences include Asian philosophy and literature. Adam Giannelli points out that the title for *The World of the Ten Thousand Things* comes from the *Tao Te Ching* attributed to Lao Tzu "who used the phrase to express the diversity of the universe."[4] The *Tao Te Ching* is one of the central texts of the Chinese practice of Taoism and offers suggestions for the proper conduct of the self in the world. Alluding to this book in his title highlights Wright's ongoing engagement with Asian texts, a connection that is more pronounced in this trilogy than it was in

Country Music. In the post–World War II period, Wright was preceded by a number of other American writers who sought religious perspectives outside Western conventions. Perhaps the Beats, who integrated Buddhist philosophies into their work, were the most memorable group, with Jack Kerouac and *The Dharma Bums* and Allen Ginsberg and "Sunflower Sutra." More contemporary with Wright is Gary Snyder, also associated with the Beats, whose long poem based on Asian influences, *Mountains and Rivers without End,* was published in 1996. Snyder's publication has several pages of oriental landscape painting inside its cover. Wright feels an affinity with Chinese poetry and art because of its focus on landscape as well (*HL* 132).

The Southern Cross

The Southern Cross marks a break with Wright's earlier books. The poet does not leave the reader with the ambiguity that he or she often finds at the end of many poems in Wright's previous collections. Instead *The Southern Cross* is full of what one interviewer calls "epiphanies." Wright responds: "Well, perhaps too much so. But I'd rather have too much of that than too little, than to have an ordered little story that leaves us thinking. 'Well, that's well written but who cares?'" (*HL* 152). These epiphanies made the book more satisfying reading for the many who came to it. At the time of its publication, Peter Stitt, for example, wrote that "*The Southern Cross* is surely Charles Wright's best book, the one he has been preparing for through all his earlier volumes."[5] Wright was becoming a better-known poet by this point, as indicated by the increasing number of reviews of his books. The one adjective repeated across various reviews of *The Southern Cross* is *original;* the word was used by such readers as Richard Tillinghast, David Young, and Calvin Bedient.[6]

David Walker called *The Southern Cross* "elegiac," but it is not elegiac in the sense that *Bloodlines* was before it.[7] The dead are again on Wright's mind as they constitute the first poem of the trilogy: "Homage to Paul Cézanne." Yet this is a more general concern with death and not directed toward specific individuals such as the elegies Wright published earlier for his parents. About "Homage to Paul Cézanne," Wright states that he had been thinking about ways to appropriate Cézanne's method that would allow him to write in a different manner than he had in his previous collection, *China Trace*. Wright admits the poem is "not about Cézanne himself, but about the process of painting" (*HL* 102). Hence, although his style may have been influenced by Cézanne's painting techniques, his subject is our relationship to the past and the way we understand those who came before us. The dead portray similar concerns as the living:

> At night, in the fish-light of the moon, the dead wear our
> white shirts
> To stay warm, and litter the fields.
> We pick them up in the mornings, dewy pieces of paper
> and scraps of cloth.
> Like us, they refract themselves. Like us,
> They keep on saying the same thing, trying to get it right.
> (*TW* 3)

Even though the dead might be imagined to have gained more insight and wisdom since they have passed over to the other side, Wright reveals they are just as clueless as any of the living when he notes they "keep on saying the same thing, trying to get it right." This is of course also what the poet does, trying to express some inner feeling but never quite getting it right, so he must continue to write on the same themes, as Wright does here about the dead, over and over again.

"Homage to Paul Cézanne" offers the reader insight into Wright's composition process. Upon the completion of *China Trace,* Wright was unsure what his next project would be, but then one evening he looked outside to see three sheets of paper on the lawn; this experience inspired him to write. He relates that he

> wrote down the line, "In the fading light the dead wear our white shirts to stay warm." Then I said, well, that's interesting. I put it down, I had supper, and then later on the moon came out, and I watched TV again, and by god those same three pieces of paper were so white that they were picking up the moonlight! And so I went back to that line and rewrote it, "At night, in the fish-light of the moon, the dead wear our white shirts to stay warm, and litter the fields." And then the next day I went out to see what they were, and they were sheets of white notebook paper from a kid's notebook. That's why they were so white. It wasn't newspaper or anything. It was blank paper! And so I worked on that particular part of the Cézanne poem for a while and got the first section. (*HL* 101)

This anecdote shows how Wright's work proceeds from observation, but then imagination takes hold: he sees the paper as ghosts, the dead, and this launches the poet on a multipart poem that is at once a meditation on his relationship to the departed, as well as a consideration of his art.

Perhaps not surprisingly, given the poem's title and Wright's well-established relationship to painting, the dead are explained using art terminology:

> The dead are a cadmium blue.
> We spread them with palette knives in broad blocks and
> planes.

We layer them stroke by stroke
In steps and ascending mass, in verticals raised from the
  earth.

We choose, and layer them in,
Blue and a blue and a breath.

(*TW* 6)

The section ends: "The dead are a cadmium blue, and they understand" (*TW* 6). The cadmium blue evokes painting in general, and "the process of painting" appears as "palette knives," which are used to layer paint thickly on the canvas.[8] Wright manipulates space and the clustering of his words and stanzas, his "tonal blocks," to gesture toward painting techniques. His couplets suggest the horizontal rhythm of landscape; notably there are no "dropped" lines in this passage. The dead "understand," since they are now elevated to the level of art; art helps them see in new ways, as it does the living.

But the speaker cannot remain confident in his pronouncements on the dead. He second-guesses himself and the role the dead play in art: "what do the dead care for the fringe of words, / Safe in their suits of milk? / What do they care for the honk and flash of a new style?" he asks (*TW* 9). The description "suits of milk" is presumably chosen for its striking image, the milky white of the original sheets of paper that inspired the poem. "Homage to Paul Cézanne" ends with "We sit out on the earth and stretch our limbs, / Hoarding the little mounds of sorrow laid up in our hearts" (*TW* 10). It is thus not clear if much has been learned from the dead if "we" continue to "hoard" our "sorrow."

The preoccupation with art in "Homage to Paul Cézanne" leads Wright elsewhere in *The Southern Cross* to consider the basic tool of his own art: language. Wright observes that "there are three things, basically, that I write about—language, landscape, and the idea of God" (*QN* 123). Though he might have demonstrated the limits of language in his poetry before, in this book Wright discusses it in the poems themselves. Such is the case in "Childhood's Body":

> It isn't enough to sing and begin again.
> It isn't enough to dissemble the alphabet
>
> And listen for
> The one heartbeat I listen for,
>
> . . . .
> My poems in a language now
>
> I finally understand.
>
> (*TW* 25)

The phrase "dissemble the alphabet" might be read as a comment on the attitude toward language adopted by such writers contemporary with Wright as the Language Poets. The radical experimentation and disjunctive poetics of this group does not appeal to Wright: "They want language as music, which is fine, but they want no I-You communication, which I find not so fine," he says about them in an interview (*HL* 150). The "I-You" connection is clearly an important part of Wright's poetics from early in *Country Music* onward. He identifies in "Childhood's Body" a desire to work against the difficult and opaque medium of language, language that he admits he only now understands and can now understand in his own poems. In this way he does reflect Language Poets such as Charles Bernstein and Ron Silliman whose main preoccupation is the function of language itself, even if Wright can disagree with what he calls the Language

Poets' "inherent lack of formal properties in their venture" (*QN* 80). Rhetorically "Childhood's Body" recalls "The New Poem" from *Country Music,* which details all the things the new poem cannot do in its strategy of negation (the repetition of the phrase "it isn't enough"). "Childhood's Body" is thus deeply concerned with the many challenges of writing, especially language usage.

The problem of poetry, and Wright's relationship to it, appears in other works in *The Southern Cross.* In "Portrait of the Artist with Hart Crane," Wright acknowledges the sameness of theme in poetry generally:

> The subject of all poems is the clock,
> I think, those tiny, untouchable hands that fold across
>   our chests
> Each night and unfold each morning, finger by finger,
>
> . . . .
>
> One day more is one day less.
>
> I've been writing this poem for weeks now
> With a pencil made of rain
>
> (*TW* 33)

Insofar as the clock might be seen to represent time and, by extension, mortality, Wright gestures to the desire for immortality common among writers. Yet the poem he writes is produced by a "pencil made of rain," and its lines will run as soon as they are committed to paper. It is the difficulty of the task of writing that Wright gets at here. In the poem preceding this one, "Dog Day Vespers," the speaker similarly notes, "I'm writing you now by flashlight, / The same news and the same story I've told you often before" (*TW* 32). The poet recognizes the sameness of his work and its message, but this does not deter him from pursuing his art, even if his art is executed in the metaphorical dark, as represented by the flashlight that must illuminate what he is writing.

Five poems in *The Southern Cross* take the title "Self-Portrait" and these poems each carry fifteen lines, recalling the form of "Skins" and "Tattoos" from *Bloodlines* that used fourteen lines. Calling his poems "Self-Portrait" continues Wright's preoccupation with the visual arts. It might be noted that painting is a subject of other postwar American poets, especially the New York School of poets that consisted of James Schuyler, Frank O'Hara, Kenneth Koch, and John Ashbery. James McCorkle mentions Ashbery's work in an essay on Wright.[9] Among the New York School, Ashbery might come closest to Wright in a preoccupation with art, especially in Ashbery's Pulitzer Prize–winning long poem "Self-Portrait in a Convex Mirror." Ashbery's poem takes Parmigianino's famous self-portrait as the basis of its meditation and reflects Wright's similar use of painting as a generative device for his own work.

Despite the implication of the poems' titles, Wright's self-portraits are not overtly autobiographical. The third one, for example, is as much about the speaker's brother as it is about himself. The fourth self-portrait consists of a catalog of Wright's favorite poets, including Dante, Catullus, Campana, and Rimbaud. The first self-portrait begins as if the speaker has a secret he is withholding: "Someday they'll find me out . . . The ashes and bits of char that will clear my name // Till then, I'll hum to myself and settle the whereabouts," and it resolves into a series of abstractions characteristic of Wright's earlier books:

> Hand that lifted me once, lift me again,
> Sort me and flesh me out, fix my eyes.

From the mulch and the undergrowth, protect me and
 pass me on.
From my own words and my certainties,
From the rose and the easy cheek, deliver me, pass me on.
(*TW* 11)

The language of salvation is apparent in the phrase "deliver me." But what the speaker means by the "rose" or the "easy cheek" is not so apparent. These references seem a personal symbolism for the speaker that holds the reader at bay.

Despite the occasional obscurities of the poems, they are also often grounded to reality in the form of landscape. There is a diversity of locations in *The Southern Cross* that is new. "Mount Caribou at Night" discusses Montana, where the Wrights have long kept a place. "Virginia Reel" evokes southern heritage and the process of generations, with its speaker seeing his place in tradition and leaving "a little vowel for the future, a signal from us to them" (*TW* 18). Murray, Kentucky, is the location of one self-portrait. California figures into the poems, especially in "Laguna Blues," which alludes to Wright's life at Laguna Beach—a location he describes as "a good place for a writer because it's so boring there's nothing to do but write" (*HL* 60). In "Laguna Blues" he combines his California life with the southern folk tradition of the blues by using a semihumorous refrain, "Whatever it is, it bothers me all the time" (*TW* 23). The refrain mimics the repetition of lines in blues lyrics. The dark and sorrowful underpinnings of this folk music contrasts sharply with the sunny setting of the West Coast.

"The Southern Cross" is Wright's tour de force at the end of the book and stands as his strongest long work to that point. J. D. McClatchy writes that "The Southern Cross" is "a very

American poem because it worries about an old world and a new."[10] The poem is broken into twenty-five parts of varying length, with sections shifting between different locations that occur in other poems of the book, especially Italy, Montana, and Tennessee. Early in the sequence Wright says, "No trace of a story line," but in the next section details of the poet's life from 1936, 1941, and 1953 prevail (*TW* 42). He writes, "How sweet the past is, no matter how wrong, or how sad. / How sweet is yesterday's noise," and memory turns out to be a persistent concern in the poem (*TW* 43). McClatchy argues, "This is not so much a man remembering as a man observing his memories."[11] The speaker of the poem seeks to make his observations universal by noting, "Everyone's life is the same life ~ if you live long enough" (*TW* 48).

Discussions of the past prove some of "The Southern Cross's" best moments:

> There is an otherness inside us
> We never touch,
>   no matter how far down our hands reach.
> It is the past,
>   with its good looks and *Anytime, Anywhere* . . .
> Our prayers go out to it, our arms go out to it
> Year after year,
> But who can ever remember enough?
>
> (*TW* 48; Wright's ellipses)

This question reverberates across the poem as the problem of remembering begins to take on the form of a crisis for the speaker. At the end of the poem the speaker seeks to return to his origin. "All we remember is wind" he says, and the next section argues:

It's what we forget that defines us, and stays in the same
 place,
And waits to be rediscovered.
Somewhere in all that network of rivers and roads and silt
 hills,
A city I'll never remember,
 its walls the color of pure light,
Lies in the August heat of 1935,
In Tennessee, the bottomland slowly becoming a lake.
It lies in a landscape that keeps my imprint
Forever,
 and stays unchanged, and waits to be filled back in.
Someday I'll find it out
And enter my old outline as though for the first time,

And lie down, and tell no one.

(*TW* 54–55)

August 1935 is, of course, the month and year of Wright's birth. In going back to his starting point, the speaker hopes to rectify the sense of disconnection he feels with the world. He could "enter [his] old outline" and through this process "rediscover" that which awaits recovery. But in the wistful way the poem is uttered ("Someday I'll find it out"), the reader realizes Wright understands the impossibility of achieving wholeness with the past.

"The Southern Cross" is a poetics of the problem of memory, but it also ironically demonstrates how much the speaker remembers. Wright remarks earlier in the poem, for example, "I can't remember the colors I said I'd never forget / On Via Giulia at sundown, / The ochers and glazes and bright hennas of each house" (*TW* 51). Yet by naming the colors, significantly identified in their painterly hues (ocher, henna), the poet reveals how much he remembers, or how much he can invent in any case, since there is no way to be sure these are the "correct" colors of the scene. In its long lines, its usage of autobiographical detail, and its multipart construction, this poem anticipates Wright's follow-up, *The Other Side of the River,* which amplifies those qualities that emerge in "The Southern Cross," especially the theme of memory.

The Other Side of the River

In a review Mark Jarman observed that "often in the past Wright's poems have hurried away from the human milieu, but in *The Other Side of the River* they are at times crowded with people."[12] As Jarman indicates, the poems of *The Other Side of the River* depart from Wright's earlier work in that new characters populate the poems, even though a few familiar figures, such as the speaker's mother who had appeared in *Bloodlines,* materialize as well. Wright explains that the new focus on people

> came about because of a review I got once, the only time, I think, that a review has been generative. Helen Vendler said there were no people in my poems, and I rather liked it that way. But there it was in print, *no people,* so I decided to put some in. I did it mostly in *The Other Side of the River,* as people seem to go best with overt narrative, and I was trying a bit of that too. Then I felt I had done it, for better or worse, and went back to where I had been before. I'm not really a people person. I'm more of a landscape person. People are mostly, for me, merely foreground for what's really going on, always behind them. (*QN* 164)

It is not surprising that Wright responds to a critique Vendler published on his work: she has long been one of Wright's most supportive readers.[13] *The Other Side of the River*'s focus on narrative and people is evident from the first poem, "Lost Bodies," in which the speaker relates a sexual encounter told to him by a man named Harold Shipley. Other narratives include "Two Stories," which narrates an encounter with a bear who inadvertently saved the speaker from sleepwalking over a cliff; "Lonesome Pine Special," the story of Solo Joe, an eccentric prospector in Montana; and "Italian Days," about a helicopter ride that almost ends in disaster. All this is to say that the storytelling is apparent, a departure from Wright's previous work.

But as with the selections from *The Grave of the Right Hand* gathered in *Country Music,* the narratives do not always prove satisfying. In the second section of "Lost Bodies," for example, the speaker begins by remembering Italy: "Torri del Benaco, on the east side of Lake Garda, / Was north past Peschiera and San Vigilio" (*TW* 60). He then writes, "One Sunday, I drove through town on my way to Riva at the top of the lake" (*TW* 60). The line creates the anticipation of a story line to follow, but all that happens is that the speaker relates a series of reveries: "I remember the cypress nods in its warm breath. / I remember the almond blossoms ~ floating out on the waves, west to Saló. / I remember the way they looked there, ~ a small flotilla of matches. // I remember their flash in the sun's flare" (*TW* 60). Even though there is certainly a stronger commitment to narrative in these poems, they do not always stick strictly to storytelling. When asked about narrative in *The Southern Cross,* Wright says, "there are different kinds of storyline, of course; there's the narrative story line, the imagistic story line, the linguistic story line, which is hardest of all, just letting the language carry it. What I tend to do is use an imagistic story line" (*HL* 142). The "imagistic story line" seems to carry through in "Lost Bodies" and other poems of *The Other Side of the River* in the vivid imagery that persists.

Yet not all the imagery in the book is tangible. "Cryopexy" reflects earlier works by Wright in its abstractness. Wright explains that the term *cryopexy* refers to a procedure to correct a torn retina that he underwent in 1981. He notes, "After they do it, they don't let you do anything for about ten days to two weeks except watch television," and he continues, "if you live in California and look up at the sky you write a poem about light, which is what this is. The entire poem is about the effects of light coming into the eye" (*QN* 130–131). The poem is filled with disorienting description and imagery that mirror the compromised senses of its speaker: "Looming and phosphorescent against the dark, / Words, always words. ~ What language does light speak? / Vowels hang down from the pepper tree ~ in their green and their gold" (*TW* 99). The strange imagery Wright employs replicates for the reader his surreal experience with weakened vision and stands as one of the more hallucinatory poems in his oeuvre.

There is a marked shift in tone in *The Other Side of the River.* Although Wright argues there is no such thing as poetry that sounds exactly like speech, the language in these poems often comes as close to ordinary speech as Wright has attempted in his career up to this point (*HL* 150). An example is "Lonesome Pine Special," which surveys different areas of the country—Kentucky, Tennessee, Idaho, Virginia, Montana, and North Carolina—by describing roads that pass through them. In discussing U.S. Route 52, Wright comments,

> Another landscape I liked
> Was south of Wytheville, Virginia, on U.S. 52
> Just short of the Carolina line,

> a steel bridge over the New River,
> Pasture on both sides of the road and woods on the easy slopes.
>
> (*TW* 69)

The chatty nature of the language ("Another landscape I liked") creates the effect that Wright is speaking directly to the reader. This constitutes quite a different strategy from that employed in the early poems in *Country Music* in which the speaker is often talking to a "you," whether it be a poet such as Ezra Pound or someone else, and the reader seems like a mere bystander. Here the address is direct. But the language heightens as the section goes on:

> What is it about a known landscape
> that tends to undo us,
> That shuffles and picks us out
> For terminal demarcation, the way a field of lupine
> Seen in profusion deep in the timber
> Suddenly seems to rise like a lavender ground fog
> At noon?
>
> (*TW* 69)

Words such as *demarcation* and *profusion* come from a different register than everyday speech. The language matches the subject: when he is speaking of everyday things, such as the look of the land and its flora, Wright uses plain language, but as his poem grows more thoughtful and philosophical, the diction similarly grows more complex.

Although painting has long been a preoccupation in Wright's work, in this book there is a concentration on a different kind of visual art: photography. Wright's wife, Holly, is a photographer, and her pictures have adorned his books, especially the photographs of the author used on the collections of his prose pieces and interviews, the first of which was published in 1988, a few years after *The Other Side of the River,* as *Halflife: Improvisations and Interviews, 1977–1987.* The photograph figures into the multipart poem "Lost Souls," where the speaker asks himself how to assess his own life, pointing out

> pictures on all the walls
> Of the way I was, and everyone standing next to me?
> This one, for instance for instance for instance . . .
>
> Nothing's like anything else in the long run.
> Nothing you write down is ever as true as you think it was.
>
> But so what? Churchill and I and Bill Ring
> Will still be chasing that same dead pintail duck
> down the same rapids in 1951
> Of the Holston River. And Ted Glynn
> Will be running too.
> And 1951 will always be 1951.
> (*TW* 65; Wright's ellipses)

As much as the speaker is talking to himself, he is also speaking to the reader, as if we were looking at the photos with him ("This one, for instance"). As is typical of Wright's work, the names of individuals who populate the speaker's memory are included in the poems, even if the names mean little to us. However, these names are not always real. For example, the teacher called Miss Sweeney (*TW* 77) in "Two Stories" is really Wright's beloved fifth-grade teacher, Miss Watkins (*HL* 149). Memories, even though Wright presents them in a realistic way, are always mediated by imagination. In its seemingly objective representation of reality, the photograph suggests that these poems present straightforward autobiography, but the details are often invented by the poet.

The mixture of reality and imagination is evident also in "To Giacomo Leopardi in the Sky," in which the speaker asks the famous Italian writer who lived long before Wright was born, "What day did I take this picture you have no part in?," and ends, "you're part of my parts of speech. / Think of me now and then. I'll think of you" (*TW* 109, 112). The speaker comes to doubt the photograph as a medium in "Looking at Pictures" where he asks, "How many times have I come here ~ to look at these photographs / And reproductions of all I've thought most beautiful / In the natural world, / And tried to enter the tired bodies assembled in miniature?" (*TW* 113). Photographs are so important to Wright that he decorates his work area with selected images. J. D. McClatchy describes the look of Wright's study during this period of his life: "Across the room from us, in a narrow dormer alcove, is his desk with its Hermes portable typewriter. Above it are photographs of his wife and of Verona, taken during his first visit there in 1959. Beside these, a drawing of Campana, and a page from an old edition of *Inferno,* Canto XXIV. 'What I look at has everything to do with what I think,' he quickly explains" (*QN* 90). The photographs work like mnemonic devices for the poet, allowing him to put himself back into a time and place, even if, as the poems show, what he sees in the photograph may need to be embellished with imaginative details.

One of the most memorable poems in *The Other Side of the River* comes near the end: "Arkansas Traveller." The title recalls "Delta Traveller," Wright's elegy for his mother in *Bloodlines.* "Arkansas Traveller" discusses different generations of Wright's family and its southern ties, but early on the poem tells specifically of his great-grandfather. Wright indicates this man "stepped off the boat ~ from the archduchy of Upper Austria" onto American soil (*TW* 105). He served in the Confederacy and was wounded at Chickamauga in his palate, the bullet Wright says he

> carried there till his death
> Almost half a century afterward.
> And wrote a poem back
> To the widow of one of his men about a sure return
> "Where life is not a breath,
> Nor life's affections, transient fire . . . in heaven's light."
> And was captured again,
> and wounded again, confined for two years
> At Rock Island prison.
> And came back to Little Rock and *began his career.*
> And died at sixty-six,
> a ticket to Cuba stored flat in his jacket pocket.
> (*TW* 106; Wright's ellipses)

The speaker then thinks of his own summers in Little Rock as a child and in the next section of playing golf with his grandmother. The poem ends,

> To speak of the dead is to make them live again:
> we invent what we need.
> Knot by knot I untie myself from the past
> And let it rise away from me like a balloon.
> What a small thing it becomes.
> What a bright tweak at the vanishing point, blue on blue.
> (*TW* 107)

Here again the reader finds the poet meditating on the dead, but there are specific individuals in mind this time—Wright's great-grandfather and his grandmother—and not the abstract or more general dead of "Homage to Cézanne." Nevertheless the dead return, as they often do in Wright's poetry, consistently working to overturn the finality of death. Within Wright's poetry the dead are our link to the otherworld, and through the process of memory we bring them back, if only for a moment.

David Kalstone said about this book that "*The Other Side of the River* is not as consistently good as its immediate predecessor, *The Southern Cross,*" but Kalstone also admits that Wright "is one of our best middle-generation poets, writing at the peak of his form."[14] Wright's technique continues to evolve in his next collection, *Zone Journals,* producing poems closer to prose than the clipped lyrics that he had published in *Hard Freight* and *China Trace.* Wright's commitment to characterization and narrative in *The Other Side of the River* also lessens in *Zone Journals.*

Zone Journals

In "The Southern Cross," Wright had begun working in a multisection composition style, and *The Other Side of the River* continued this approach although the length of his lines grows. *Zone Journals* capitalizes on both of these innovations as Wright's poems are often very long in terms of sections and line length: "A Journal of the Year of the Ox" is the longest at forty-one pages. The poems all use the word *journal* in their titles and thereby highlight the free-flowing nature of the writing. This "journal entry" style offers Wright the advantage of poems that feel more process-oriented as result, where importance is placed on capturing the writer's thoughts in the moment and offering them seemingly unmediated to the reader; Wright points out that valuing process in writing is indeed one of the main reasons for this approach (*QN* 111).

Wright's manner of looking at his work was changing as well. Around this time he speaks of an "American sprawl of a poem with a succession of succinct checks and balances. Epiphanic and oceanic at once. Intensive and extensive," and he concludes, "Now *that*'s American" (*QN* 116). The "sprawl" of *Zone Journals* is evident in its diversity of subject and its form. In terms of subject, the poems vary widely, from recounting the speaker's time in England and Italy, to discussing the wrongs committed against the Cherokee tribe in the South. Wright remarks in an interview that *The World of the Ten Thousands Things,* in terms of form, was "retroactive structurally" (*QN* 169). What he means by this is that after he had completed *Zone Journals,* he came to view the earlier volumes in the trilogy as similarly journallike in nature. This perspective certainly makes sense for most of *The Other Side of the River* and some poems of *The Southern Cross*—the title poem, in particular.

Mark Jarman praised the metaphysical leanings of *Zone Journals* by noting, "Wright's metaphysics is truly inclusive, as paradoxical as that may sound. Inclusion—the proliferation of detail and image—is what he and C. K. Williams and Philip Levine have in common."[15] Not all reviewers were impressed with the poems of *Zone Journals.* William Logan wrote, "Some of Mr. Wright's critics would make him a visionary, but his talent is ill-suited for that. His best work has always been founded in the hard-edged fact, not the gauze of metaphysics."[16] Logan concludes, "he has never managed to write the one book that would lift his reputation over that of his peers. 'Zone Journals' may be slave to that ambition, and in it what earlier seemed great gifts have become merely talent straining for effect."[17]

The long lines and the occasional mysticism of *Zone Journals* were anticipated in the work of one of the celebrated American poets of the nineteenth century: Walt Whitman. Not surprisingly, in *Zone Journals,* Wright sounds more like Whitman than ever before. In an interview Wright discusses his "longtime ambition to be Emily Dickinson on Walt Whitman's open road," and thus he combines the "mother" and "father" of modern American poetry in his work (*QN* 172). The poems of *Zone Journals* marry the focus on imagery in Dickinson with the "sprawling" lineation of Whitman. Echoes of Whitman can be detected in "A Journal of True Confessions": "If you want to hear me, you'll have to listen again. / You'll have to listen to what the wind says, ~ whatever its next direction" (*TW* 141). These lines can be compared to Whitman's at the end of "Song of Myself": "I bequeath myself to the dirt to grow from the grass I love, / If you want me again look for me under your boot-soles."[18] In both texts the speaker has been incorporated into nature, and the reader is directed to look for him there.

As is usual in Wright's books, the speaker does a good deal of traveling: both to actual locations and through his memories. Although Italy appears quite often in *Zone Journals,* as it had in the books that preceded it, a new locale is England. This setting is captured in "A Journal of English Days," where the speaker spends some time accompanied by his wife in locations such as Kensington Gardens. References to English writers including Sir Phillip Sidney and John Keats abound, as well as old favorites of Wright's such as Pound, who had lived for some time in London. The date and location of the poem, "London 1983," are provided at its end, and the sections are distinguished by month, going from September to December (*TW* 134). Early in the poem the speaker experiences an epiphany: "I suddenly recognize / The difference between the spirit and the flesh ~ is finite, and slowly transgressable" (*TW* 125). *Zone Journals*—in fact *The World of the Ten Thousand Things* overall—does not depict the kind of transcendence that Wright intimates here; that comes more in *Negative Blue.* Nevertheless he does arrive at other conclusions, such as "there is no sickness of spirit like homesickness / When what you are sick for ~ has never been seen or heard / In this world, or even remembered ~ except as a smear of bleached light" (*TW* 131). There is a spiritual longing in these lines, a sense heightened later in the poem by the speaker's assertion that "God is an abstract noun" (*TW* 134). "A Journal of English Days" concludes with Wright and his wife in a courtyard with a Buddha at one end and the sound of "the faint hiss of eternity" (*TW* 134).

The Asian influence that surfaces with the Buddha at the end of "A Journal of English Days" is carried through in "Night Journal," which presents the phrase that serves as the title of this trilogy:

> —Everyone wants to tell his story.
> The Chinese say we live in the world of the ten thousand
>   things,
> Each of the ten thousand things
>   crying out to us
> Precisely nothing,
> A silence whose tune we've come to understand,
> Words like birthmarks
>
> (*TW* 147)

The silence the speaker identifies is cited in other places in the book. The poet is confronted with a silence to which he must listen closely to hear the "tunes" that give him his poems. Many of the poems in the book appropriate a haiku-like approach in which the poet is listening to—and looking at—nature. An example can be found further on in *Zone Journals,* in "Chinese Journal," where Wright observes, "Inside their bristly circle, / The dwarf boxwood ~ flashes its tiny shields at the sun" (*TW* 199).

A sense of futility, and perhaps despair, haunts the speaker of "A Journal of One Significant Landscape":

> One of the nondescript brown-headed black birds that yawp
> And scramble in and out of the trees
>   latches me with his lean eye
>
> And tells me I'm wasting my time,
>   something I'm getting used to
> In my one life with its one regret
> I keep on trundling here
>   in order to alter it.
> You're wasting your time, he tells me again. And I am.
>   (*TW* 195)

Although wasting one's time is generally viewed negatively in society, it does not have to be read that way here. The idea that the speaker is "wasting [his] time" might be from the perspective of a culture that does not value meditation and philosophical insight, which one could argue the West does not. The speaker's retreat to Eastern philosophy shows his desire to find a tradition that appreciates his thirst for spiritual clarity. The only way he can attain enlightenment is through "wasting" his time in meditation.

The title of the centerpiece of the book comes from the practice of naming years after the constellations of the Chinese zodiac:

"A Journal of the Year of the Ox." Whereas "A Journal of English Days" had named actual months of the year, "A Journal of the Year of the Ox" goes even further and offers specific dates on which sections were completed, running from January to December. The poem chronicles a single year of writing, 1985. Not only does the writing during this period appear journal-like in its prose-influenced style, but the dates appended to the parts of the poem create the sense that the sections have been lifted straight out of Wright's journal and are direct reflections of his thought processes as he considers his experiences.

"A Journal of the Year of the Ox" is one of the longest individual poems in the trilogy of trilogies and unique in a couple of ways. For one, it introduces the importance of the Blue Ridge Mountains that are the locus of many meditations in *Negative Blue* (*TW* 150). The Blue Ridge Mountains, part of the Appalachians running from Pennsylvania to Georgia, cross through Wright's home in Charlottesville, Virginia. "A Journal of the Year of the Ox" is also unique in its subject: several sections focus on the plight of the Cherokee in Tennessee. The last section on this Native American tribe, however, reports that land had been returned to them by the city of Kingsport in 1976. Kingsport was one of Wright's boyhood homes, and thus the poet acknowledges the troubles of the town, as well its attempt to rectify past grievances.

The problems of language that surface as a motif in the beginning of the trilogy in such poems as "Childhood's Body" carry into this book as well. In "Night Journal," Wright states, "Words, like all things, are caught in their finitude" (*TW* 149). Language is similarly one of the concerns of "A Journal of the Year of the Ox," in which Wright declares,

In the rings and after-chains,
In the great river of language that circles the universe,
Everything comes together,
No word is ever lost,
                    no utterance ever abandoned.
. . . .
                                   there is a word, one word,
For each of us, circling and holding fast
In all that cascade and light.
Said once, or said twice,
                    it gathers and waits its time to come back
To its true work:
               concentrate, listen hard.

(*TW* 176)

The idea that there is "one word" for "each of us" shows the speaker desires the denotative profusion of language to cease and so he "listen[s] hard" for an answer. Slightly later in the poem, while "gazing at the Madonna," the speaker searches for *his* word:

Only this silence, the strict gospel of silence,
                                             to greet me,
Opened before me like a rare book.
I turn the first page
                    and then the next, but understand nothing,
The deepening twilight a vast vocabulary
I've never heard of.
I keep on turning, however:
                    somewhere in here, I know, is my word.

(*TW* 177)

And yet his one word fails to materialize, despite his listening closely to the "silence." The poet even evokes his own words, such as when he thinks of "those I would be among, / The called, the bruised by God" near the end of the poem (*TW* 184). This line echoes "Clear Night" from *China Trace* in which the speaker declares, "I want to be bruised by God / I want to be strung up in a strong light and singled out" (*CM* 152). The desire to be close to God in *China Trace* persists in "A Journal of the Year of the Ox's" speaker, so much so that he cannot even find new language with which to speak of his desire in *Zone Journals* but must repeat the "bruised by God" motif.

The problems of language persist up to the end of the book, where Wright writes, "To find one word and use it correctly, ~ providing it is the right word, / Is more than enough" (*TW* 200). This search for the "one word" pushes the poet on, even if he knows it is likely futile. If he were to find this one word, he would presumably stop writing. That does not happen, and the nature of words and language continue to be a concern in *Xionia*.

Xionia

With *The World of the Ten Thousand Things,* Wright begins a practice that carries into *Negative Blue*. That is, he finishes the trilogy by adding on a short collection of poems—what Wright calls a "coda"—that had been first printed separately as a chapbook.[19] As with other chapbooks, a format that poets often turn to as a way of presenting material that is not of sufficient length for a full-length collection, this book was published on a limited basis, using techniques and materials that typically do not go into mass-produced books. *Xionia* consisted of "250 signed copies printed by hand from Joanna types on either Johannot or

Iyo papers, case bound, quarter cloth, paper over boards," as described by Christopher Buckley.[20]

J. D. McClatchy explained the title *Xionia* in a review: "The term is a private name Wright and his wife gave the house they bought some years ago in Charlottesville. The former owners had named the house—because of its architectural detail—'Ionia.' Wright wittily unnamed it by x-ing the old term, while at the same time savoring the echo of Zion."[21] In naming the chapbook after his home, Wright makes a symbolic gesture, welcoming readers into his life and his point of view.

Xionia carries on *Zone Journals*'s practice: each poem bears the word *journal* in its title, although these poems are generally shorter than those in *Zone Journals.* "A Journal of the Year of the Ox's" preoccupation with language appears here as well. Wright specifically addresses contemporary theoretical views of language in the aptly named "Language Journal": "Maybe the theorists are right: ~ everything comes from language. . . . But I don't think so today, ~ unless the landscape is language / Itself, which it isn't" (*TW* 217).[22] One of the theorists Wright has in mind is presumably Jacques Derrida, the French philosopher, whose theory of deconstruction wielded a large influence on literary studies in the 1970s and the 1980s. Derrida explores how the binaries through which Western thinking proceeds—light versus dark, male versus female, speech versus writing—can be shown to be faulty. Language proves to be a method of communication laced with problems in Derrida's thinking, always on the verge of falling apart. He argues that if one looks at language closely, one sees that words are arbitrary agents to which meaning is assigned and that they are at times at cross-purposes with one another. Wright responds to this line of thinking, "The verb that waits for us in the trees ~ is reconstruct, not deconstruct" (*TW* 217). He thereby repudiates the deconstructionist view of language by focusing on "reconstruction," not "deconstruction." Elsewhere he quips, "A deconstructionist critic writing about Language Poetry is like a dog eating its own vomit" (*QN* 80).

One of the twentieth century's leading poets concerned with the fragmentation of language and one of Wright's longstanding influences, Ezra Pound, is evoked in "A Journal of Southern Rivers." Wright indicates that, after almost forty years of writing, his concerns are enduring:

> What lasts is what you start with.
> *What hast thou, O my soul, with Paradise,* for instance,
> Is where I began, in March 1959—
>   my question has never changed,
> Always the black angel asleep on my lips.
>   (*TW* 224)

The italicized phrase is the first line from "Blandula, Tenulla, Vagula" by Pound, the poem that inspired the beginning of Wright's writing career when Wright was in the army in Italy. It is a "black angel" on the speaker's lips because he is willing to ask the difficult questions of God and theology, just as Pound was fearless in being his own poetic thinker.

Along the lines of the divine, *Xionia* introduces a concept of paradise that the poet had not directly addressed before. "May Journal" reads,

> The visible world is nothing more than a trompe l'oeil
> By someone wanting a moment's peace
> From the knowledge that Paradise

is what we live in

And not a goal to yearn for.

(*TW* 221–222)

By this point in *The World of the Ten Thousand Things,* it could be surprising for the reader to find Wright rejecting the "visible world" as a "trompe l'oeil." After all, so many of the poems are given over to describing nature and landscape. The book ends with "Out of our own mouths we are sentenced, ~ we who put our trust in visible things" (*TW* 230). There is still a spiritual thirst in the speaker, despite his realization that paradise does not likely exist beyond what he sees. Yet the speaker's desire for transcendence continues in the next collection, *Negative Blue.* The location Wright mentions for the first time in *The World of the Ten Thousand Things* at its very end, in *Xionia*—Charlottesville, Virginia—is central to *Negative Blue* as it proves the setting for the speaker's philosophical speculations that mark the final section of his long work (*TW* 221). The focus on the earthly in *The World of the Ten Thousand Things* gives way to an even greater commitment to spiritual matters in *Negative Blue,* and thus the final trilogy seeks to reflect the "Tomorrow" and "Up There" aspects of the "Yesterday, Today and Tomorrow / Down There, Here and Up There" model the poet settled on for his trilogy of trilogies.[23]

CHAPTER 4

On *Negative Blue*

Published in 2000, *Negative Blue: Selected Later Poems* constitutes the final section of Wright's long poetic project and includes *Chickamauga* (1995), *Black Zodiac* (1997), *Appalachia* (1998), and the chapbook *North American Bear* (1999). In an interview with Ernest Suarez, Wright describes how he sees this last group of books following the plan of *Country Music,* in this case with *Chickamauga* as the inferno, *Black Zodiac* the purgatory, and *Appalachia* the paradise, again based on Dante's *Divine Comedy.*[1] But later Wright told Daniel Cross Turner that after *Chickamauga,* "*Black Zodiac* was the second book, which would have been the purgatorial part. *Appalachia* was the final book, the book of the dead, since I couldn't write a *Paradiso.* The reason *Appalachia* was called *Appalachia* was because *Chickamauga* was called *Chickamauga,* which is to say that each title has four syllables. *Black Zodiac* also has four syllables. These are silly reasons, but it had something to do with it."[2] This explanation shows how fluid Wright's project has been: whereas Wright wanted *Appalachia* to be the "paradise," imitating Dante's cosmology, he could not quite make it that. Instead he calls it a "book of the dead"; a book, in other words, focused on the afterlife but not necessarily paradise. Wright's counting the number of syllables in the titles indicates his desire for symmetry, as well as his attention to language. As mentioned, Wright counts syllables even within his poetic line, usually using an odd number to avoid falling into a conventional metrical pattern.

For the reader used to the "American sprawl" of Wright's journal-entry style in *The World of the Ten Thousand Things* (1990), *Negative Blue* requires some adjustment. The poems of *Negative Blue* retain the long, "dropped" line that Wright had been perfecting in *The World of the Ten Thousand Things,* but the poems are not nearly as lengthy or as sprawling; instead they are much more self-contained than the poems in Wright's previous trilogy. *Negative Blue* thus merges the looser lineation of *The World of the Ten Thousand Things* with the briefer poems of *Country Music* (1982). In *Negative Blue* the two impulses find their resolution. *Black Zodiac,* however, stands apart from the other two books in its extensive use of multipart poems, thereby more resembling the second trilogy than the first. In general Wright's strategy in *Negative Blue* is that if poems relate to one another (such as "The Appalachian Book of the Dead" series that makes up part of *Appalachia*), he allows them to share a title, and he numbers them (for example, his pair of poems "Venexia I" and "Venexia II"), rather than create poems with multiple sections such as past works including "The Southern Cross."

During this period Wright was the recipient of further distinctions. In 1993 he received the Ruth Lilly Poetry Prize for lifetime achievement; in 1996 he won the Lenore Marshall Prize from the Academy of American Poets; the National Book Critics Circle Award for poetry was awarded to him in 1997; and in 1998 he was named the Pulitzer Prize winner in poetry for *Black Zodiac.* Correspondingly reviews for *Negative Blue* were strong, with Ashley Brown noting Wright's project as "one of the most ambitious poems of our time" and comparing it to Pound's *Cantos* and Berryman's *Dream Songs.*[3] Ron Smith named Wright a "poet's poet" with the publication of the collection, and M. L.

Schuldt wrote that *Negative Blue* contained "some of the most unforgettable lines" of Wright's career.[4] Christina Pugh called the book "a satisfying retrospective of Wright's most recent work."[5]

Despite the critical praise for the book, it is not without its challenges. The title of this trilogy is perhaps the most obscure of the three. What could be meant by "negative blue?" The color blue appears throughout the poems, in various guises. Blue can of course represent the sky, called "blue zones" at one point (*NB* 116), to which Wright's speaker so often looks, and it might be "negative" because he never sees God's outline in the clouds like he would wish. There are many specific references to blue: the angels' "blue wings" (*NB* 46), the "blue moan of the mourning dove" (*NB* 47), the "blue blank page" (*NB* 89), and "God's blue breath" (*NB* 134). There is "Cicada Blue," which carries the refrain "blue, I love you, blue" (*NB* 157). Wright evokes the southern musical tradition of the blues in "Poem Almost Wholly in My Own Manner" and "Giorgio Morandi and the Talking Eternity Blues."

Ron Smith writes, "*Negative Blue* is a great hymn to a divinity-deprived earth—and to the forms of language the mind shapes so gloriously and yet ultimately ineffectually to its shifting contours."[6] The color blue, and the poems in which references to it occur, is reflective of the general mood of the work that J. D. McClatchy points out is "a sustained meditation on mortality."[7] With such a somber task in front of the poet as producing a "great hymn" that nevertheless focuses on "mortality," perhaps no color better than blue would capture the vision of the world he puts forth, given the color's association with pensiveness, reflectiveness, or unhappiness.

The "negative" in the title might also be explained as Wright's theology, as Henry Hart illustrates: "In *Negative Blue* and in poems collected in earlier books, Wright frequently espouses a central tenet of the apophatic or 'negative theology' inherent in most mysticisms—that God can only be approached through a *via negativa,* a purging of the mind's cognitive and linguistic functions and that God can only be hinted at through negative statements delineating what He is not. From the perspective of negative theology, God is an absence, a wholly 'other' nonbeing; representations that affirm His presence, in fact, misrepresent Him."[8] Mysticism forms an important part of this trilogy as Wright cites the well-known mystic William Blake (*NB* 40) and Julian of Norwich in the poems (*NB* 81).[9] Hart's interpretation of Wright's mystic-inspired view of God is helpful in understanding the multiple perspectives taken on God in *Negative Blue.* If God is understood through negation, then Wright's sometimes seemingly atheistic statements might be regarded as paradoxically supporting the existence of God. In any case, by the end of *Negative Blue* the speaker's relationship with God remains unclear. Yet this complicated relationship is the source of many poems and begins first in *Chickamauga.*

Chickamauga

The title of this book is drawn from the famous Civil War battle in 1863, in which the army from Tennessee helped bring about a Confederate victory and drove the Union back to Chattanooga, Tennessee, from Chickamauga, Georgia. As Helen Vendler indicates, "it is typical of Wright's practice" that details of the actual battle appear nowhere in the title poem.[10] Wright notes that he chose the title because "that's where my great-grandfather was wounded out of the Civil War and I wanted to have some connection, some familial connection with that particular volume, since I had the Dante trilogy in mind."[11] His poem "Arkansas Traveller" from *The Other Side of the River* had told the story of this great-grandfather's involvement in southern history. In the same interview Wright also claims, "I always wanted to have a book with a Southern title, so I picked *Chickamauga* and on the front of the book there's a picture my wife took of me saying 'Chickamauga.'"[12]

In general the titles of Wright's poems in this trilogy are more inventive than before, even if they are also less explanatory for the reader, as in the case of "Chickamauga." By contrast, in *Zone Journals* (1988), as with other earlier works, the titles carry a service-oriented, if somewhat bland, quality. The reader knows what he or she is getting in a poem titled "A Journal of English Days," for example. But in poems called "Still Life on a Matchbox Lid" and "After Reading Tu Fu, I Go Outside to the Dwarf Orchard," what the reader will encounter in the poems is not so obvious. Titles in *Chickamauga* are also sometimes comical, such as "Miles Davis and Elizabeth Bishop Fake the Break"—one does not usually associate the great jazz trumpeter and bandleader with the troubled poet. "An Ordinary Afternoon in Charlottesville" clearly echoes Wallace Stevens' celebrated poem "An Ordinary Evening in New Haven." More nonsensical titles include "Blaise Pascal Lip-Syncs the Void," which Wright humorously indicates is "the most serious title I've ever written" (*QN* 125). In the short essay "Titleism," Wright ironically says that "the proper title *is* the poem," and in an interview he affirmed that his titles during this period are much more playful than before: "All you have to do is teach writing for a little while, and you know how helpful titles are. You ask people, 'Well, what is this about?' and the title has nothing to do with it. So, of course, now I'm doing exactly what I tell them not to do. The title has nothing to do with these poems" (*QN* 28, 159–60).

Although the title poem of *Chickamauga* does not directly address the battle after which it is named, the poem does deal with history generally when Wright argues, "History handles our past like spoiled fruit" (*NB* 33). It is thus the problems of history that bother the speaker here—the idea that history may not adequately represent the past, and poetry is similarly problematic: "The poem is a code with no message" (*NB* 33). Near the end of "Chickamauga," Wright warns, "The gill net of history will pluck us soon enough / From the cold waters of self-contentment we drift in / One by one ~ into its suffocating light and air" (*NB* 33). The speaker's general dissatisfaction with history and the ability of his medium, poetry, to communicate a message appears in the metaphor of fish being drawn from the sea, "suffocating" on land as he suffers the ill effects of history.

Part of the problem of history may derive from the poet's culture. Wright explains in an interview, "the South means a great deal to me. The look of it, the 'idea' of it, the history of it as I knew it," but then he admits, "Of course, it's not really 'The South' anymore. Television killed all that in the homogenizing of America. All our character has become caricature now. TV did what Grant and Sherman never could: it finally ended the war. In most senses, of course, that's a wonderful thing. The 'burden' seems gone that Faulkner, for instance, wrote under and out of" (*HL* 181). Although the South has lost some of its differences from other parts of the country, Wright emphasizes that this homogenizing impulse in American culture is not wholly a negative force. He indicates that the burden of southern history, presumably its long tradition of racial discrimination, has been eased by mass media. But he also worries about the passing of local identity, which is rooted in a sense of the past. Wright has always been quick to acknowledge that he is a *southern* poet, although he hopes to be more than "merely a Southern poet" (*HL* 159).

One of the key elements of the South is its strong religious background. But Wright's relationship to religious materials takes a different form in this trilogy. The poet is increasingly invested in mysticism, as Henry Hart shows. In *The World of the Ten Thousand Things,* Jesus appears in the first poem in *The Other Side of the River,* "Lost Bodies." Here the speaker relates a sign he passed daily while living in Kingsport, Tennessee: "GET RIGHT WITH GOD / JESUS IS COMING SOON" (*TW* 59). The religious slogan represents a clear example of the evangelistic spirit Wright remarks was also part of his schooling (*QN* 145). In *Chickamauga,* on the other hand, the figure of Jesus is of another kind:

> Jesus said,
> Lift up the stone and you will find me,
> Break open a piece of wood, I'm there.
> It's hard to argue with that,
> Hard to imagine a paradise beyond what the hand breaks.
> (*NB* 54)

This image of Jesus is drawn from the Nag Hammadi Library, a collection of fourth-century texts that were recovered after World War II in Egypt. The texts depict a different Jesus, one who in the lines Wright paraphrases speaks for his presence everywhere, not just in church. Wright evokes saying 77 in the *Nag Hammadi*'s Gospel of Thomas ("Lift up the stone and you will find me, / Break open a piece of wood, I'm there").[13] In saying 3, Jesus declares, "the kingdom is inside of you, and it is outside of you."[14] This is a Jesus who directs his followers to seek a personal connection with the divine, not mediated by the church;

he certainly is not advocating evangelism. In this way it is easy to see why the Jesus of the *Nag Hammadi* appeals to Wright, who tends in his poems to question conventional religion and views of God but seeks God still.

Elsewhere in the book, the speaker identifies an unnameable spiritual presence in nature:

> Something surrounds us we can't exemplify . . .
> . . . .
> We hear it at night.
> Flake by flake,
> we taste it like tinfoil between our teeth.
>
> Under the little runnels of snow,
> under the mist
> settling like moonlight
> Over the orchard,
> under the grasses and black leaves,
> In its hush, in its sky width, it takes our breath away.
> (*NB* 27)

These lines come from "Sprung Narratives," a poem evocative of such earlier works as "A Journal of the Year of the Ox" in that it is built through short sections and carries some narrative and nonnarrative passages. The poem begins by relating an anecdote about the speaker and his brother as boys, shortly after the end of World War II. Then it shifts to the speaker's past in Italy and forward to his life spent in Laguna Beach, California. He draws attention to the anonymity he experienced in California living: "I walked among them, booted, black-jacketed, peering / Unsurreptitiously into ~ whatever was recognizable. / I never knew anyone" (*NB* 25). It is later in the poem that he reaches the section that indicates that "something surrounds us." By that point in the text, the speaker's mystical perspective helps to link together the disparate experiences he relates, with the speaker finding some salient metaphysical impulse in the different settings of Tennessee, Italy, and California. In moments such as these in *Negative Blue,* Wright is able to make what would be unresolved fragments in his earlier work into more satisfying reading with a stronger sense of unity, governed by the speaker's ongoing search for the divine.

But for all the poems' discussions of spirituality or mysticism, there is what seems to be a persistent doubt of God in *Chickamauga.* Early in the book, in "Cicada," he writes, "We measure what isn't there. / We measure the silence. ~ We measure the emptiness" (*NB* 15). The emptiness here does not have to be read as God; in fact it could be an allusion to a Buddhist sense of emptiness in all things; the reader cannot be sure. However, later in the collection, in "The Silent Generation," there appears to be less ambiguity: "We walk up and down in the earth, ~ we take our flesh in our teeth. / When we die, we die. The wind blows away our footprints" (*NB* 37). The admissions that we "measure the emptiness" and "when we die, we die" presents a world seemingly marked by an absence of God. But Wright contends that "everything hinges on doubt. Without a beginning in doubt, there is no faith. Thomas is the main man here. Without Original Doubt there is no future acceptance" (*QN* 167). It is thus possible, and perhaps advisable, to see Wright's speaker as a perpetual "doubting Thomas."

James Longenbach wrote in a review at the time of the book's publication that "I sometimes found myself wishing that *Chickamauga* didn't seem quite so world-weary quite so often."[15] This "world-weariness" appears in some poems in the form of the poet's questioning the fruits of his labor: "Hard work, this business of solitude. / Hard work and no gain," he laments at one point (*NB* 55). Early in the book, in "Reading Lao Tzu Again in the New Year," the speaker contends,

> Desire discriminates and language discriminates:
> They form no part of the essence of all things:
>
> each word
>
> Is a failure, each object
> We name and place
> leads us another step away from the light.
> (*NB* 5)

The denotative and connotative slipperiness of language that Wright had written about at the end of *The World of the Ten Thousand Things* reaches a conclusion here where words themselves are "failure[s]" and lead one only further from "the light," which can be taken as an emblem for knowledge or enlightenment.

The poems are also concerned with the poet's mortality to a degree not evident in Wright's work before, as J. D. McClatchy has noted. In "Under the Nine Trees in January," the speaker remarks, "The world is a handkerchief. / Today I spread it across my knees. / Tomorrow they'll fold it into my breast pocket, ~ white on my dark suit" (*NB* 6). The speaker views himself after death, as he is being dressed in his dark suit for burial. An emphasis on mortality is also evident in "After Reading Tu Fu, I Go Outside to the Dwarf Orchard": "Day after day, I become of less use to myself. / Like this mockingbird, ~ I flit from one thing to the next. / What do I have to look forward to at fifty-four?" (*NB* 12). There is a pervasive sense of loss and futility in these lines. The speaker takes comfort in the idea that he will become what he has written so much about:

After it's over, after the last gaze has shut down,
Will I have become
The landscape I've looked at and walked through
Or the road that took me there
or the time it took to arrive?
(*NB* 24)

Yet for all the uncertainties of the future and the afterlife, the poet has his ongoing mission: the abiding long poem. "I gaze at the sky and cut lines from my long poem," he writes further on in the book (*NB* 30). John Berryman, whose *The Dream Songs* Wright acknowledges as an influence (*HL* 172), jokingly writes, "The only happy people in the world / are those who do not have to write long poems."[16] The long poem has the been pursuit of almost every major American poet after Walt Whitman: Ezra Pound's *Cantos,* William Carlos Williams's *Paterson,* H.D.'s *Trilogy,* Robert Lowell's *History,* the list could go on. Wright self-consciously places himself into that venerable, but arduous, twentieth-century tradition.

The speaker's work in poetry also offers him some solace against the inevitability of death. The book ends with a consideration of the immortality of writers in "Yard Work." It begins, "I think that someone will remember us in another time, / Sappho once said—more or less—"and the speaker replies, "I hope so, myself now caught / Between the edge of the landscape and the absolute, / Which is the same place, and the same sound, / That she made" (*NB* 67). But the speaker decides that whether he will be remembered is not for him to decide; instead he says, "My job is yard work— / I take this inchworm, for instance, and move it from here to there" (*NB* 67). For all the poems' investment in metaphysics, the earthly has the final say in the book, in the form of a worm. But it is clear that the poet's pursuit of those abstractions "landscape and the absolute" will continue, and indeed they do, in what is one of Wright's most acclaimed books: *Black Zodiac.*

Black Zodiac

Wright's Pulitzer Prize–winning collection, *Black Zodiac,* is book-ended by two extended poems, "Apologia Pro Vita Sua" and "Disjecta Membra," that recall the longer pieces in *The World of the Ten Thousand Things.*[17] Not only do these poems carry on the sectional divisions of such earlier poems as "A Journal of English Days," but they also use narrative to distinguish themselves from most of the other poems in *Black Zodiac,* which are more meditative and image-driven than they are narratively constructed. The other poems in the book also tend to be shorter, but all of *Black Zodiac*'s poems, regardless of length, share the strong sense of closure prevalent first in the work collected in *Chickamauga.*

In "Apologia Pro Vita Sua" ("A Defense of His Life"), Wright offers insights of various kinds: into the landscape, into spirituality, and into the nature of memory. Section 2 begins, "Something will get you, the doctor said, ~ don't worry about that. / Melancholia's got me. . . . I'm sick and tired of my own complaints" (*NB* 76). Some of the "world-weariness" that Longenbach complained of in *Chickamauga* appears here, although the poet admits he has grown tired of his own preoccupation with melancholy. In fact Calvin Bedient objected to Wright's persistent melancholy early on in Wright's career. Bedient noted that this mood prevented Wright's poems from attaining much variance in tone.[18] Now the poet expresses his own weariness with that mood.

The speaker's melancholy might be seen as a product of his view of the past, which is rooted in memory. Wright says in an interview that once a memory is embellished by imagination it is "grooved in forever" and will not change (*QN* 163). The problem of memory's disconnection with reality is the subject of one section of "Apologia Pro Vita Sua." The speaker relates how during summer camp, when he was sixteen, he would watch his roommate,

> A college guy, gather his blanket up, and flashlight,
> And leave for his rendezvous with the camp cook—
> he never came back before dawn.

After the reverie, the speaker shares a later encounter with the roommate:

> Some 40 years later I saw him again for the first time
> Since then, in a grocery store, in the checkout line,
> A cleric from Lexington, shrunken and small. Bearded even.

The surprising appearance of the man forces the speaker to confront what he had established in his memory and elaborated upon with his imagination:

> And all these years I'd thought of him, if at all, as huge
> And encompassing,
> Not rabbit-eyed, not fumbling a half-filled brown sack,
> dry-lipped, apologetic.
> (*NB* 77)

The speaker has trouble squaring his memory with the reality he faces. Is the man "shrunken and small" because of age? Is it because of his vocation? As a cleric, perhaps he did not live the full, earthly life that seemed promised to him, as represented by his youthful rendezvous with the camp cook. The poem can be interpreted as making an argument for the problem of the religiously devoted, where the man has seemingly been diminished ("dry-lipped, apologetic") by his choice of profession. The speaker, too, in what might be called his "secular devotion" to poetry and mysticism might be seen as having missed out on what life had to offer. His time is similarly devoted to the realm of the spirit and not the flesh.

Despite what seems a mind for detail in such sections as the roommate turned cleric, the speaker notes later in "Apologia Pro Vita Sua" that "there is a forgetfulness in me which makes me descend / Into a great ignorance," though he admits, "what I remember remains" (*NB* 82). Thus the speaker may have forgotten many details along the way, but that which he has always remembered stays strong, even if those memories are not always supported by reality, as he finds with the cleric. Memory is figured as a positive force in the poem, as Wright indicates later: "What I remember redeems me, ~ strips me and brings me to rest" (*NB* 83). The speaker finds his redemption in memory despite what forgetfulness may dodge him.

Other narratives appear in section 2 of "Apologia Pro Vita Sua," perhaps most notably one marked by the speaker working as a collection officer for a bank, "bringing more misery to the miserable," he ruefully recounts (*NB* 79). The section ends poignantly with the speaker returning to the issue of mortality. This time he thinks of mortality in terms of more than his own short time on the earth, but of others' as well:

> My parents' 60th wedding anniversary
> Were they still alive,
> 5th of June, 1994.

It's hard to imagine, I think, your own children grown
  older than you ever were, I can't.

I sit in one of the knock-off Brown-Jordan deck chairs
  we brought from California,
Next to the bearded grandson my mother never saw.
Some afternoon, or noon, it will all be over. Not this one.
(*NB* 80)

The lines comment not only on the speaker's own mortality, but also his departed parents' and eventually his son's. The speaker stresses the importance of savoring the moment as he knows all that seems permanent in the present will eventually pass away. The image of the speaker in a simple, suburban lawn chair appears throughout the trilogy. Like the persistent images of dogs in *Country Music,* the motif works to ground the poems in the everyday, the mundane.

Wright has continued to search for the divine in the world, and in *Black Zodiac* landscape is presented as a tool for that process: "Landscape's a lever of transcendence— ~ jack-wedge it here, / Or here, and step back, / Heave, and a light, a little light, will nimbus your going forth," Wright decides (*NB* 71). Insofar as landscape may lead to transcendence, the speaker is also cautious in how fervently he believes in his power to attain that "going forth" into transcendence. He reveals, "I've had these for forty years, ~ light-prints and shifting screed, / Feckless illuminations" (*NB* 81). His illuminations might very well be divinely inspired visions, but he is quick to point out they are also "feckless," imperfect.

The writing style that the poet employed in *The World of the Ten Thousand Things*, the journal, is linked with his pursuit of landscape in "Apologia Pro Vita Sua": "Journal and landscape /

—Discredited form, discredited subject matter— / I tried to resuscitate both, breath and blood, ~ making them whole again // Through language" (*NB* 72).

In his use of the term *resuscitate,* the speaker sounds like Ezra Pound in "Hugh Selwyn Mauberley," who famously declares, "For three years, out of key with his time, / He strove to resuscitate the dead art / Of poetry."[19] Wright similarly discusses the frustrations he faces in using a poetic style inspired by journal writing and in trying to discuss landscape in new ways. Like Pound, he will continue to pursue what he feels is right, although Wright's pursuit is more spiritual than Pound's ever was.

Elsewhere Wright speaks directly to Pound. In the first of the series of "The Appalachian Book of the Dead" poems (the rest of which appear in the next volume, *Appalachia*), Wright includes the quote "*Go in fear of abstractions . . . ,*" which is drawn from Pound's "A Retrospect"—a series of suggestions and rules for poetry writing (*NB* 99). Wright responds to the quote: "Well, possibly. Meanwhile, / They *are* the strata our bodies rise through, the sere veins / Our skins rub off on" (*NB* 99). Wright's hesitancy to leave behind abstractions is not surprising: much of his poetic career has comprised writing that is either blatantly abstract or on the verge of becoming abstract. In fact his love for abstraction is encoded in his response to Pound: can the reader imagine bodies rising through strata? The trope is too abstract to form a strong image in the reader's mind. But in the next stanza Wright does follow Pound's advice and the poem grows more concrete:

> Uneasy, suburbanized,
> I drift from the lawn chair to the back porch to the
>   dwarf orchard
> Testing the grass and border garden.

The speaker in his chair and then in the orchard are tangible images; more so, in any case, than the bodies in the strata. But then the poem grows abstract again:

> A stillness, as in the passageways of Paradise,
> Bell jars the afternoon.
>
> (*NB* 99)

This is a favorite strategy of Wright's in *Negative Blue:* balancing the poems between the real and the imagined, the tactile and the metaphorical, the abstract and the concrete. A variation on this strategy can be observed in "Meditation on Song and Structure." In this poem Wright discusses birds indigenous to the different landscapes he loves: first the mourning dove in Virginia, then the nightingale and swallow in Italy, the mockingbird in North Carolina, and finally the cardinal with the speaker presumably back in Virginia. The birds bring landscape and memory together. Like the motif of the speaker in his backyard, they give the poem everyday detail.

The backyard figures so much in these poems that Willard Spiegelman uses the phrase "backyard metaphysics" to describe Wright's approach.[20] In "Disjecta Membra" ("Scattered Parts") the reader finds,

> Back yard, dry flower half-border, unpeopled landscape
> Stripped of embellishment and anecdotal concern:
> A mirror of personality,
> unworldly and self-effacing,
> The onlooker sees himself in,
> a monk among the oak trees . . .
>
> (*NB* 129)

The backyard is admitted to being a mirror for the speaker. It reflects his concerns and his personality, which prefers an "unpeopled landscape." He admits to himself, however, "How silly, the way we place ourselves—the struck postures, / The soothing words" (*NB* 129). There is a self-reflexive quality here to Wright's work that is new. The poet had never quite so deliberately reflected on himself, nor did he draw attention to his method before. This new self-consciousness helps the speaker avoid some of the world-weariness of the other poems. When he says later in the poem, "Whatever it was I had to say, ~ I've said two times, and then a third" he is directly addressing criticism the reader might have of his limited thematic range (*NB* 138).

The book's ending finds the speaker looking attentively to the future:

> Take a loose rein and a deep seat,
> John, my father-in-law, would say
> To someone starting out on a long journey, meaning, take it easy,
> Relax, let what's taking you take you.
> I think of landscape incessantly,
> mountains and rivers, lost lakes
>
> . . . .
>
> I'm emptied, ready to go. Again
> I tell myself what I've told myself for almost thirty years—
> Listen to John, do what the clouds do.
>
> (*NB* 141)

Though clearly making reference to the speaker's literal life journey since the book has been consistently engaged with the notion of mortality, this passage also gestures to the speaker's other journey: his ongoing long poem. Even though he may have a plan in mind for its direction, he must attend his father-in-law's advice and "let what's taking you take you." The poem must grow organically; the poet may want to write paradise, but he might not be able to do so. It is in this way that Wright sets the stage for the trilogy's final volume, *Appalachia*.

Appalachia

In a review James Longenbach observed that "*Appalachia* is Wright's least garrulous book since *China Trace*."[21] *Appalachia*'s poems tend to be short—almost all fit on one page—and thus contrast with *Black Zodiac*'s, which includes the long works "Apologia Pro Vita Sua" and "Disjecta Membra." In terms of the book representing the "paradise" in Wright's scheme, the poet relates, "Appalachia is the exact opposite of what one might think of as a paradisal place, but, growing up in it, I loved it. I tend to think of western North Carolina, eastern Tennessee, southwestern Virginia, that part of Appalachia, as containing heavenly aspects, which I know is not true for most people, but they were for me. This again comes back to all the landscape business. You think about what's behind it, but you're left with what you can see."[22] The use of the title, *Appalachia,* and Wright's explanation of it show how hard the poet has worked to be regarded as a southern writer. He admits that he is not usually thought of in that way because his poems generally eschew narrative, narrative often being viewed as central in southern verse. In fact Wright has expressed frustration with the assumption that a southern poet must be narratively driven many times in interviews (*QN* 150).

But like *Chickamauga,* which has little to say directly about the Civil War battle after which it is named, little is explicitly said about Appalachia in the book, aside from the descriptions and meditations on landscape that persist. The first poem of the book, "Stray Paragraphs in February, Year of the Rat" declares:

East of town, the countryside unwrinkles and smooths out
Unctuously toward the tidewater and gruff Atlantic.
A love of landscape's true affection for regret, I've found,
Forever joined, forever apart,
outside us yet ourselves.
(*NB* 145)

The tone is wistful—by now a familiar Wright trait:

Renunciation, it's hard to learn, is now our ecstasy.
However, if God were still around,
he'd swallow our sighs in his nothingness.
(*NB* 145)

Wright admits in "Halflife: A Commonplace Notebook" that "all my poems seem to be an ongoing argument with myself about the unlikelihood of salvation" (*HL* 37). The part of the poet who believes in the possibility of salvation appears to be losing the argument in this poem as Wright is as direct as he ever has been in writing that God is no longer "still around." Yet even this statement is ambiguous: is Wright saying people no longer believe in God, or is God simply absent, withdrawn from the world but persisting somewhere else? The poem does not answer these questions directly, but the speaker's address to the month during which he is writing, February, asks for a reprieve from the spiritual loneliness he feels:

February, old head-turner, cut us some slack, grind of bone
On bone, such melancholy music.
Lift up that far corner of landscape,
there, toward the west.
Let some of the deep light in, the arterial kind.
(*NB* 145)

Light, as often in Wright's poems, is figured as the salvation the speaker awaits. This is a deep light, one which, when it arrives, will be what the speaker has longed for.

Despite an ambivalence about spiritual matters that continues in the book, some poems in *Appalachia* are filled with a sense of finality. "Basic Dialogue" is one of these, as the speaker says, "I think / I'll lie down in the dandelions, the purple and white violets. / I think I'll keep on lying there, one eye cocked toward heaven" (*NB* 147). The speaker waits for his time for release; as he says in the preceding poem, "Stray Paragraph in April, Year of the Rat," "If we were to walk for a hundred years, we could never take / One step toward heaven— ~ you have to wait to be gathered" (*NB* 146). The speaker appears, however, to have run out of patience in being "gathered" and requests,

> Now is the time, Lord.
> Syllables scatter across the new grass, in search of their words.
> Such minor Armageddons.
> Beside the waters of disremembering,
>   I lay me down.
>
> (*NB* 147)

The use of the address "Lord" and the final two lines in the poem echo perhaps the best known of all the Psalms, 23: "The Lord is my shepherd; / I shall not be in want. He makes me lie down in green pastures / and leads me beside still waters." It is significant the speaker lays himself down; the Lord does not do it. The speaker still hopes that salvation can be his in this time of "minor Armageddons" when language is disjointed ("syllables . . . in search of their words").

"Ars Poetica II" rebuts "Basic Dialogue" by its admission that "I find, after all these years, I am a believer," which surprises the reader with what seems to be a definitive statement on the speaker's relationship to faith. But the speaker is quick to add qualifications: "I believe what the thunder and lighting have to say; / I believe that dreams are real" (*NB* 156). God in this poem appears a positive force: "God is the fire my feet are held to" (*NB* 156). God challenges the speaker; one might even say he inspires the speaker. The title of the poem refers to the practice of a poet writing a poem about writing poetry, an ars poetica. The question then is whether God is a metaphor here for the poem or for art generally? Is it within God that art resides; or is it the other way around: is God to be found in art?

This quality of *Appalachia*—the tendency for its poems to knot into unsolvable philosophical quandaries—was noted by Adam Kirsch. In a review of the book, he wrote that "for all the agitation in Wright's style and mood, the poems in *Appalachia* have very little forward motion. Each of them returns to the same problem, the same dilemma, and comes away with the same frustration: Wright is 'waiting for something to come—anything,' but it never does. And while this monotony is not a defect, a sign of the poet's lack of skill, it is nonetheless a limitation."[23] Kirsch then noted that "it is a limitation that stems, ultimately, from Wright's very conception of what poetry should do"—that is, replicate philosophical tension.[24] For readers such as Kirsch, this is a shortcoming of the book and Wright's approach generally: "It is this refusal—the unwillingness to live without so much, both spiritually and poetically—that condemns the poems in *Appalachia* to turn continually upon themselves, allowing them neither sort of consummation. Yet it is also a product of Wright's particular integrity, and what makes his poetry such a significant and true reflection of our time."[25] Kirsch finds the value of Wright's poetry in his refusal to create solutions to the complex problems his work explores. In this way Kirsch sees Wright reflecting the questioning nature of his times. If Wright were to produce poems that simplified their complicated subjects, the poet would not retain the same integrity in Kirsch's eyes, as well as those of many of his readers.

Not all the poems, however, display the unresolved uncertainty that Kirsch describes. The focus on photographs that emerged in *The Other Side of the River,* for example, returns in "In the Kingdom of the Past the Brown-Eyed Man is King." The photograph, or rather what it is emblematic of (self-aggrandizement), forms the focus of the speaker's critique:

> It's all so pitiful, really, the little photographs
> Around the room of places I've been,
> And me in them, the half-read books, the fetishes . . .
> . . . .
> Who do we think we're kidding?
>
> Certainly not our selves, those hardy perennials
> We take such care of, and feed, who keep on keeping on
> Each year, their knotty egos like bulbs
> Safe in the damp and dreamy soil of their self-regard.
> (*NB* 151)

J. D. McClatchy speaks of the "lush musicality" of Wright's poetry,[26] and that may be as apparent in the last line as anywhere in Wright's work: the repetition of sibilants striking against the *d*'s in "damp," "dreamy," and "regard" provide the line with an inner cohesion and a sense of balance. The poem ends by noting, "The country of *what was,* the country of *what we pretended to be,* / Cruxes and intersections of all we'd thought was fixed. / There is no guilt like the love of guilt" (*NB* 151). The speaker admits his wallowing in "guilt" here is really a preoccupation with self—that "knotty ego." Ultimately, then, although he is aware of his problem he cannot solve it.

The most important sequence of *Appalachia* is "The Appalachian Book of the Dead," comprising six numbered poems—the first of which appears in *Black Zodiac*—as well as the other poems in *Appalachia* in which this fictional book is cited: "The Writing Life," "Giorgio Morandi and the Talking Eternity Blues," "Early Saturday Afternoon, Early Evening," and "After Rereading Robert Graves, I Go Outside to Get My Head Together." The "Appalachian Book of the Dead" poems operate as others in the book do: they are set in Charlottesville, with the speaker performing a kind of meditation in his backyard as the world goes on around him. In "The Appalachian Book of the Dead II," for example, "Children are playing their silly games / Behind the back yard, ~ toneless, bell-less Columbus Day" (*NB* 162); in "The Appalachian Book of the Dead V" the speaker is "half-asleep on the back deck, ~ low wasp-hum of power mower / Ebbing and coming back from next door" (*NB* 181). These are images of what Wright calls, in "A Bad Memory Makes You a Metaphysician, a Good One Makes You a Saint," "our landscape, / Bourgeois, heartbreakingly suburban" (*NB* 149). They are everyday scenes, "heartbreaking" in their simplicity but also in their search for material comfort—the "bourgeois" existence, which everyone, including the speaker, takes for granted.

Yet like the text the title is borrowed from—the ancient Egyptian Book of the Dead that included instructions for the afterlife—this book of the dead discusses more than the everyday; it is also concerned with such weighty subjects as the longing of the soul:

Jerusalem, I say quietly, Jerusalem,
The altar of evening starting to spread its black cloth
In the eastern apse of things—
        the soul that desires to return *home,* desires its own
            destruction,
We know, which never stopped anyone,
The fear of it and dread of it on every inch of the earth,
Though light's still lovely in the west,
                                        billowing, purple and scarlet-white.
(*NB* 162)

As with Wright's early work, light appears as a symbol of salvation, although this light is notably purple and tinged with scarlet. It is not the typical white light found in religious paintings and instead bears colors associated with Christian motifs: the scarlet reflects the blood of Christ and the purple his passion. The evocation of the city holy for Christians—Jerusalem—and the apse, the place for the altar in the church, defines this book of the dead in strictly Christian terms. It is a book in which the soul seeks that which could bring about "its own destruction."

Wright makes passing reference to "The Appalachian Book of the Dead" throughout the poems, but, in "After Rereading Robert Graves, I Go Outside to Get My Head Together," Wright carries on a discussion with Robert Graves in a way similar to his evocation of Ezra Pound and Chinese poets earlier in the trilogy and offers the reader some perspective on the nature of this particular book of the dead. Graves's well-known study of mysticism in poetry, *The White Goddess,* is the subject of Wright's meditation:

According to Graves, the true function of poetry
Is a strict, religious invocation of the Muse.

Tell it to the Marines, Roberto,
the Muse is as dead as God is.
In memory of the Muse, perhaps—
In memory of a Memory: a hidden face, a long, white veil.

And yet The Appalachian Book of the Dead exists,
In part, to ease an exit, praise the present and praise the past.
(*NB* 186)

"The Appalachian Book of the Dead" can be seen standing in the face of the fact that magic is gone from the world (the muse is dead) and religion is on the decline. In "After Reading T'ao Ch'ing, I Wander Untethered through the Short Grass," the speaker similarly declares, "Religion's been in a ruin for over a thousand years. / Why shouldn't the sky be tatters, ~ lost notes to forgotten songs?" (*NB* 183). Although "The Appalachian Book of the Dead" can help us "praise the present and praise the past," it can also "ease an exit," whether that is interpreted as our exit from this world, the exit of religion from our lives, or our loss of hope in the muse (who represents art). In any case it is a tool for transcendence.

Adam Giannelli has suggested that this title, "The Appalachian Book of the Dead," will be applied to all of the trilogy of trilogies by Wright's readers.[27] Wright himself somewhat hesitantly has adopted this title.[28] To apply "The Appalachian Book of the Dead" to other works in Wright's long poetic project is to see them in a new light. It presents a common theme for the trilogies that was more clearly evident in certain volumes than others: death. The dead are a major part of *Bloodlines,* but much less so in *The Other Side of the River,* which is more centered on life. Most of Wright's books nevertheless are elegiac in tone or content—often both. Over the years Wright's focus on this theme has varied from speaking of the passing of specific individuals, including his parents, to a more general dead as in "Homage to Paul Cézanne." The issue of mortality and how we are remembered after we die has consistently been one of Wright's paramount concerns.

The title "Appalachian Book of the Dead" also reinforces the sense that it is a basically mystical endeavor Wright undertakes, trying to engage the divine directly, using the tools at his disposable: the land he knows well as a southerner, often figured as the abstraction "landscape," and language, his primary tool as a poet. Insofar as the title might be ironic as with many of Wright's *Negative Blue* titles—ironic in the sense that Appalachia is popularly perceived to be a materially and culturally deficient area of the country, and yet Wright seemingly elevates it to the level of a culture as revered as ancient Egypt—offers a distinctly self-aware tone to the rest of his oeuvre, although the reader surely does not have to read all the works with the same perspective. If one does adopt this point of view when reading Wright's earlier work, the sometimes overearnestness of his early poems, such as his invocation of Pound in "Homage to Ezra Pound," for example, or his pronouncements in "The New Poem," are flavored with a tongue-in-cheek wisdom that questions the poet's own authority. Likewise the poet's career-long mystical search might be questioned, but it is not necessarily repudiated, through the title's ironic nature.

North American Bear

Wright completes *Negative Blue* by attaching seven poems originally published under the title *North American Bear.* These poems follow the one-poem-per-page style of *Appalachia.* The self-awareness that emerged in *Negative Blue* appears here as well. After the first two poems—"Step-Children of Paradise" and "Freezing Rain"—both of which use stars as central images, the third poem, "Thinking about the Night Sky, I Remember a Poem by Tu Fu," ends,

> Useless to let the mind grind down
> To what's beyond it.
> I'll set my sights on something small, I'll finish this poem,
> This one that's not about the stars,
> but what's between them.
> (*NB* 195)

Stars are a common symbol in Wright's work, often appearing generically but also in specific references to constellations such as the Southern Cross and Orion. Each of the three major parts of the *Divine Comedy* ends with Dante mentioning the stars, and surely this is one motivation for Wright to use them as well. The self-consciousness that emerges elsewhere in *Negative Blue* is evident in Wright's desire to "set [his] sights on something small," which simply turns out to be "finish[ing] this poem." In the final poem of this short collection, Wright returns once more to the stars and makes a distinction between human-made lights and stars, which he calls "arterial pulse of ground lights and constellations" (*NB* 201).

The strongest poem of *North American Bear* is the title poem. Early on the speaker describes himself as "a sixty-two-year-old, fallow-voiced, night-leaning man, / I stand at ease on the blank sidewalk" (*NB* 196). These lines mimic William Butler Yeats's in his poem "Among School Children" in which, as the title implies, the speaker visits pupils in a primary school: "The children's eyes / In momentary wonder stare upon / A sixty-year-old smiling public man."[29] Yeats's figure is smiling and a "public man" whereas Wright's inhabits the "night" and is "fallow-voiced." Yeats's poem ends with the philosophical paradox, "How can we know the dancer from the dance?," which can be interpreted in a number of ways.[30] From the perspective of Wright's work, the line might imply that one cannot tell the speaker from his visions; what he does ("the dance") is irrevocably tied to what he is ("the dancer").

Yeats shared Wright's love of mysticism and in his book *A Vision* attempted to present a view of the interconnectedness of the spiritual and physical worlds. "North American Bear" finds Wright continuing with his own mystical visions:

> What is it about the stars we can't shake?
>   What pulse, what tide drop
> Pulls us like vertigo upward, what
> Height-like reversal urges us toward their clear deeps?
> Tonight, for instance,
> Something is turning behind my eyes,
>   something unwept, something unnameable,
> Spinning its line out.
> Who is to say the hijacked heart has not returned to its cage?
> Who is to say some angel has not
>   breathed in my ear?
>
> (*NB* 196–97)

The speaker's hope for transcendence, "something" that could be an angel breathing in his ear, persists here as it has in previous poems. The passage brings to mind the "something surrounds us we can't exemplify, something / Mindless and motherless" lines from *Chickamauga* where the speaker identifies a metaphysical presence but cannot necessarily decide what it is.

Despite his insight into that which cannot be explained in the world, the speaker nonetheless cannot shake the preoccupation with mortality that runs throughout the trilogy: "How bright the fire of the world was, I think to myself, / Before the white hair and the ash of days. / I gaze at the constellations, ~ forgetting whatever it was I had to say" (*NB* 198). Finally, the speaker determines, "There is a final solitude I haven't arrived at yet, / Weariness like a dust in my throat" (*NB* 198). He resolves he "feel[s] safe, as the stars spill by, for one more night / Like some medieval journeyman enfrescoed with his poem in his hand, / Heaven remaining my neighborhood" (*NB* 198). Heaven remains the speaker's "neighborhood" insofar as he continues to search for the divine. Heaven here, of course, could also refer to the stars on which he has had his eye fixed for so many poems. When asked if he has "a system of belief," Wright responds, "No. I have a system of nonbelief. I would love to be a believer. But I'm not. And that's why everything always ends at the stars, at the heaven of the fixed stars."[31] Wright's description of the fixed stars is reminiscent of the ending of *China Trace,* where the main figure is frozen in "the Heaven of the Fixed Stars," "a man-made heaven" as Wright describes it (*HL* 30). But, in the context of the poem, the stars can also be a divine destination, a knowledge of which eludes the speaker as he continues on as a "journeyman."

North American Bear ends with the speaker describing "such sidebars, such extra-celestial drowning pools / To swallow us. ~ Let's lie down together. Let's open our mouths" (*NB* 201). Notably this surrendering to the "extra-celestial" is offered as an invitation to the reader; Wright asks us to pursue these matters with him further. Wright's investigation into the earthly and the divine, and the meeting place of the two in his poems, continues into three subsequent books: *A Short History of the Shadow, Buffalo Yoga,* and *Scar Tissue.* These volumes show that the themes of the trilogy of trilogies were not depleted with the publication of *Negative Blue* and that the dropped-line poetic style that had served Wright throughout his career would be of further use in his post-trilogies work.

CHAPTER 5

On Later Books

At the time of the publication of *Appalachia,* James Longenbach wrote, "Charles Wright's trilogy of trilogies—call it 'The Appalachian Book of the Dead'—is sure to be counted among the great long poems of the century."[1] After the completion of this extended poetic project, Wright published three more books that he sees corresponding to his earlier work: *A Short History of the Shadow* (2002), *Buffalo Yoga* (2004), and *Scar Tissue* (2006). He says, "Both *A Short History of the Shadow* and *Buffalo Yoga* are a diminuendo for the trilogy of trilogies, which for lack of a better title has been referred to as *The Appalachian Book of the Dead. Scar Tissue,* the new book, is the end of all that stuff."[2] For Wright these three books offer a dropping off of intensity from the trilogy of trilogies, as revealed by his use of the musical term *diminuendo,* a decrease in volume. The reader finds that these volumes, which Wright also calls "the long goodbye" to the Appalachian Book of the Dead project, carry on many of the same themes as the earlier work.[3] Spirituality continues to be an abiding preoccupation, as does art, especially in the form of painting, as well as the problems of memory, the work of the imagination, the vicissitudes of place, and the importance of family heritage. The elegiac mood evident early in Wright's career persists in these collections as well. From *A Short History of the Shadow* to *Scar Tissue,* the reader finds that Wright's primary concerns endure and the books carry on the general approach of *Negative Blue.*

A Short History of the Shadow

The speaker in "Lost Language" from *A Short History of the Shadow* declares, "I have a thirst for the divine" (*SH* 20). Thus Wright announces in his first post-trilogy of trilogies book that the search to understand the divine that has driven him over the last three decades continues. The book was generally well received by reviewers such as Jay Parini, who wrote in the *Nation* that Wright was "sifting the world before him with astonishing freshness."[4] *Publishers Weekly* called the book a "moody, winning collection."[5] But others—such as Lee Oser, who wrote, "Wright's poetic vision does not satisfy his own deepest needs"—identified in the work a philosophical search that Wright's poetics of inconclusiveness could not always satisfy.[6]

The book begins with a series of poems taking the title "Looking Around." Wright explains his approach in this series: "The first part of *A Short History of the Shadow* was a coming down from this long project that I did, my Appalachian Book of the Dead. There are three sections. One had to do with this room, my study. One has to do with the back yard. And one has to do with Montana. Those are the three places I tended to write those three books of *Negative Blue* in. That's what 'Looking Around' means. After that, the poems seem to me somewhat different. A 'project' doesn't underlie everything that I write, as it used to."[7] The settings of Wright's meditations do not change from what the reader is accustomed to in *Negative Blue;* his study, his backyard in Charlottesville, his cabin in Montana—these continue to be the launching pads for Wright's exploration of nature and the divine, but the attitude of the speaker has changed. "Looking Around III" starts in typical Wright fashion, with the speaker's detailing the Montana landscape, looking "beyond the south meadow and up the attendant feeder hills," but he admits, "I find I have nothing to say to any of this" (*SH* 9). This sense of malaise goes on until the end of the book, where Wright notes in the last poem, "Body and Soul II," "Getting too old and lazy to write poems, ~ I watch the snowfall" (*SH* 78). More than ever, the speaker feels unable to find insight in nature, even though the reader might expect that after so many years of study of the natural world, the speaker would have plenty to say about it. The speaker says laziness and old age prevent him from writing poems, but of course this is not true: the frequency with which Wright published books only increased over the years; it did not diminish. Between the time of *Chickamauga* and *Scar Tissue,* seven books were published in eleven years, compared to the period of *The World of the Ten Thousand Things,* which witnessed four individual volumes in nine years.

It turns out Wright does have something to say, after all. At the end of "Looking Around III" he writes,

> To look hard at something, to look through it, is to
>   transform it,
> Convert it into something beyond itself, to give it grace.
> For over 30 years I've looked at this meadow and
>   mountain landscape
> Till it's become iconic and small
> And sits, like a medieval traveler's triptych,
>   radiant in its disregard.
>
> (*SH* 11)

By his looking, the speaker has transformed the landscape. He has conferred grace on many things over the years. Preeminent among them is the landscape, and though it may be diminished (made "small") by his looking, it is also now iconic. Like religious icons, the speaker's visions are filled with a spiritual power and are radiant in nature.

The speaker's trouble in finding something to say appears elsewhere in *A Short History of the Shadow.* In "The Secret of Poetry," Wright describes the difficulty of the poet's job. He begins, "The second Chinese said, all that you need to find poetry / *Is to look for it with a lantern,*" but he contends that "it's hard to find, / Despite what the Chinese said. / It's hard to find despite what the moonlight jukes and joins" (*SH* 24). Ultimately he decides, "The north wind in the bare limbs of the oak trees bears down on us. / The song of the north wind fills our ears with no meaning" (*SH* 24). Wright produces a paradoxical situation: is not deciding that something has no meaning an indication of taking meaning from it? If the speaker looks into landscape, looks into his own art, looks into God and sees only emptiness, is this not insight? In any case, the fact that he continually embarks on these exercises suggests that the speaker holds out the possibility that he will eventually find a final "meaning" after all.

In "Night Rider" the speaker admits his tendency to find more contentment in what he imagines than in what he actually sees in front of him.[8] His dissatisfaction may be rooted in the inability of the natural world to live up to what he can create with his own imagination:

> I think it's all incomprehensible,
> Everything that we look at.
> Much easier, I think, to imagine the abyss, just there,
> The other side of the hedge,
> than to conjure the hedge,

The trees, and time like a puddle of water and not a stream.
Below me, red-clay Rivanna, river of Lethe
I cross and re-cross each day.
The world, I think, was made by mistake.
Perishable, mortal.
It is like us, its children, pale and predictable.
Unlike the abyss, such black, such immortal water.

(*SH* 30)

It is significant that "I think" punctuates the speaker's assertions here. He is qualifying himself, not at all unquestionably confident in his perspective. The Rivanna he speaks of is a river near Charlottesville. As in previous volumes, Wright uses the features of his region (here, the Rivanna) to tie his poems to a particular location. Drinking from the river Lethe, one of the rivers of Hades in Greek mythology, caused forgetfulness. Elsewhere in his work Wright discusses the problems of memory, especially in "The Southern Cross," and here too the forgetfulness of the speaker is evoked.

Negative Blue began employing humorous titles that Wright admitted had little to do with the poems, and that tradition carries into *A Short History of the Shadow* and to a lesser degree into *Buffalo Yoga* (*QN* 159–60). By the publication of *Scar Tissue,* only a few such titles persist. Those in *A Short History of the Shadow* are often based on everyday phrases such as "If My Glasses Were Better, I Could See Where I'm Headed For," "It's Dry for Sure, Dry Enough to Spit Cotton." One also finds examples such as "If This Is Where God's At, Why Is That Fish Dead?" and "Why, It's as Pretty as a Picture" in the book. The ironic or humorous nature of the titles contrasts with the serious content of the poems. The titles offer Wright a way to bring playfulness into his work without sacrificing serious philosophical inquiry. They show he is self-conscious in his approach to the poems and does not naively undertake his forays into theological speculation.

Although the titles of the poems of *A Short History of the Shadow* recall those of *Negative Blue,* there are also stylistic innovations in the book. One recurring strategy is the use of comparisons between nature and popular culture. In "Lost Language," Wright speaks of "sunlight thin as Saran Wrap" (*SH* 20). The title poem remarks on the "Orange Crush sunset over the Blue Ridge" (*SH* 39). The last poem of the book describes an "afternoon sky the color of Cream of Wheat" (*SH* 78). As with the titles, the descriptions reveal the speaker self-consciously constructing his poems. These descriptions ground the speaker's understanding of nature in images or products so common in contemporary American popular culture that they form a shared vocabulary. In terms of style, *A Short History of the Shadow* also carries a unique repetition of phrases not common in Wright's other books. In "Looking Around III," one finds the phrase "I don't understand" recurs (*SH* 10); in "Charlottesville Nocturne" Wright repeats "it has been said" (*SH* 17); in "Night Rider," "Nothing prepares" appears several times (*SH* 29). These repetitions give a new sense of rhythm to the poems and call to mind the similar use of repetition among one of Wright's enduring influences, Walt Whitman in "Song of Myself."

Also like Whitman, Wright continues to find inspiration in the landscape. Curiously Wright is not usually described as a nature poet.[9] This may be because his abstractions and search for God overshadow his descriptions of nature. Yet Wright often discusses the natural world in provocative ways, as in this except from "Is" in which he describes the change from winter to spring:

March is our medicine,
                    we take it at morning, we take it at night.
It, too, is colorless, it, too, is cold and past tense.
But it's here, and so are we.

Each waits for deliverance.
March, however, unlike ourselves, knows what to expect—
April again in his Joseph coat.

The seasons don't care for us. For them,
                    transcendence is merely raiment,
And never a second thought.
Poor us, they think, poor us in our marly shoes,
                    poor us in our grass hair.
(*SH* 32)

The phrase "April again in his Joseph coat" suggests the fullness of color of the month after spring has arrived. Wright associates the changing of season with transcendence and notes how matter of fact it is for the natural world to transform every season. Humans try to change too but are ultimately part of the earth—a fact underscored by the personified months observing people as having marly, or clay, shoes, and grass for hair. The speaker hypothesizes that perhaps our transcendence is already coded into our beings, and if we could recognize in ourselves what nature recognizes in us, we would be better off.

It is no surprise to see religious motifs appear in *A Short History of the Shadow* after seeing them used so consistently in Wright's other work. Perhaps what is surprising is the degree to which Wright's early life as an acolyte in the Episcopal Church still influences his thinking. In "Polaroids," he comments,

Our world is of little moment, of course, but it *is* our world.
Thus it behooves us to contemplate,

from time to time,
The *weight of glory* we should wish reset in our hearts,
About the things which are seen,
and things which are not seen.
(*SH* 33)

The phrase "things which are seen, ~ and things which are not seen" evokes the Nicene Creed, spoken during Episcopal services, which reaffirms the congregation's beliefs:

We believe in one God,
The Father, the Almighty,
Maker of heaven and earth,
Of all that is, seen and unseen.[10]

Wright's memory of these lines testifies to the degree to which he was inculcated by church and that he still at least partially understands the world through its perspective. Later in the poem he speaks of "postbelief," but nevertheless the speaker is clearly inextricably marked by his exposure to church culture (*SH* 35).

A Short History of the Shadow may be Wright's most past-poet haunted book since *Hard Freight*. Within its pages the reader finds references to Campana (*SH* 8), Mandelstam (*SH* 9), Ovid (*SH* 27), Hardy (*SH* 27), Dante (*SH* 39), Lorca (*SH* 40), Cavalcanti (*SH* 43), Stevens (*SH* 47), Pound (*SH* 68), and Blake (*SH* 75), among others. It is little wonder in a book that often, as with much of Wright's late work, makes use of language, words, and syllables as metaphors that the poet feels a need to reference his influences so consistently. The speaker focuses on the nature of language, for example, in "Via Negativa," where he contends that "words are dust, and everyone's lip that uttered them is dust" (*SH* 62). Further on in the poem he says,

> The verbal hunger, the narrowness
> Between the thing itself and the naming of the thing
> Coils like a tapeworm inside us
> and waits to be filled.
> (*SH* 63)

Wright's description of a "verbal hunger" and its parasitic nature figured as a tapeworm does not offer a positive image for the life of the writer and his or her obsession with language. The lines hint at the struggle of articulation and the search for meaning that is apparent in the book from early on. The speaker places himself in the long tradition of poets who are attracted to language, but he admits that it is not necessarily a harmless attraction. This sense of conflict persists into Wright's next volume, *Buffalo Yoga,* which like earlier collections, such as *Bloodlines,* proves deeply elegiac. Unlike *A Short History of the Shadow, Buffalo Yoga*'s conflict centers more on the difficulty of loss than the problems of language and literature, and stands as one of Wright's darkest books in mood.

Buffalo Yoga

In terms of the length of its poems, *Buffalo Yoga* is a mixture of the different approaches taken throughout Wright's career: it features some brief poems reminiscent of the short sections of *China Trace;* a longer, multipart title poem forms the center of the book and mirrors such earlier works as "The Southern Cross," "A Journal of the Year of the Ox," and "Apologia Pro Vita Sua" in its structure; and the mid-length poems that dominate *Negative Blue,* especially *Appalachia,* are represented here. Wright's ongoing concern with art, especially painting, appears in poems such as "Homage to Mark Rothko" (whose painting appears on the book's cover) as well as "Homage to Giorgio Morandi."

Michael Scharf's review of the book in *Publishers Weekly* was typical of the critical reception of *Buffalo Yoga:* "Wright's real subject, as always, is larger than it seems: though they may vary little from poem to poem, his extended, loping lines project a patient point of view that, like a kind of stretch that sometimes releases painful histories, continues to open space."[11] Many readers feel as Scharf does, that Wright's poems vary little in style or tone, but nevertheless in their spiritual searching offer the potential for fresh insights. Richard Rand noted that, with *Buffalo Yoga,* Wright's poems "become more transparent, a little less hermetic. He now offers plenty of elbow room with space for both his own and the reader's imagination."[12]

Buffalo Yoga continues *Negative Blue*'s abiding concern with the mortality of the speaker. This theme surfaces in the book's complex title poem:

> All my life I've listened for the dark speech of silence,
> And now, every night,
> I hear a slight murmur, a slow rush,
> My blood setting out on its long journey beyond the skin.
> (*BY* 10)

The speaker prepares himself for his departure from the earth, that "long journey beyond the skin" that awaits him. As with the end of Pound's *Cantos,* a sense of finality pervades the work: "May the past be merciful, ~ the landscape have pity on me— / Forgive me my words, forgive me my utterances" (*BY* 13). These lines echo Pound's final fragments of *The Cantos* in which he says, "Let the Gods forgive me what I / have made / Let those I love try to forgive / what I have made."[13] Like Pound's speaker,

Wright's senses that he must ask for forgiveness. There are other echoes of poets in the book, such as John Berryman in "Rosso Venexiano" and T. S. Eliot, whose lines from "The Love Song of J. Alfred Prufrock" ("I have heard the mermaids singing, each to each. // I do not think that they will sing to me")[14] are mimicked in Wright's "Charles Wright and the 940 Locust Avenue Heraclitean Rhythm Band": "The stars have opened their bottomless throats, and started their songs. / They are not singing to us, / It turns out, they are not singing their watery songs to us" (*BY* 55). The poet's mortality is tied up with the immortality he seeks in verse, even though he, like Pound's speaker in *The Cantos,* may not be exuberant with confidence in what he has achieved.

There are ghostly presences throughout "Buffalo Yoga." The reader finds "God's ghost taps once on the world's window" (*BY* 9); "A dead face appears at the window, then disappears" (*BY* 11); "half-remembered / Faces roll back, stripped of their foliage, / To haunt their bodies, ghost-gazed and newly peregrine" (*BY* 19). The descriptions are also dark, even by Wright's standards: "How beautiful summer is, ~ unclottable darkness / Seeping across the landscape / Like blood from a hemophiliac" (*BY* 20). Further on the speaker says, "Our lives are the length of a struck match, / And our days are sure to end in a dark confusion" (*BY* 20). If one turns to *Buffalo Yoga* for comfort against sorrow and the demands of the world, he or she is unlikely to find it. These poems are at times bleak in their outlook.

But they can also be deeply moving, as when the title poem evokes the death of a specific individual: Tom Andrews. Andrews was a poet who had edited *The Point Where All Things Meet* (1995), the first collection of reviews and essays on Wright's work, which was subsequently revised and enlarged by Adam Giannelli as *High Lonesome* (2006). Andrews died young, of a coma he fell into while in Greece.[15] Wright's notes in the back of the book list Andrews's birth and death dates as 1961–2001. The speaker of "Buffalo Yoga" discusses the discovery of a water ouzel's nest, a bird that is able to walk under water to search for food, and reflects that he

> thought of Tom, just dead in a foreign land,
> And wanted to be an ouzel myself and walk
> under the North Atlantic
> And bring him back, and lay him in the stiff, mossy bed
> Forever, above the water,
> to walk in which is a wondrous thing
> In either world, in either station.
>
> (*BY* 18)

The image of the speaker walking under the Atlantic to bring back the body of his friend is deeply affecting. Wright speaks of Andrews once more near the poem's end, writing,

> Black dog and golden dog at large in the meadow marsh.
> They are burying Tom in West Virginia, and that is that,
> Butterfly back at the dandelion,
> as cosmopolitan as the weed.
>
> (*BY* 21)

The reader identifies the speaker's sad resignation in the flat statement "they are burying Tom in West Virginia" and the helpless comment, "that is that." The poem concludes,

> The world is a magic book, and we its sentences.
> We read it and read ourselves.
> We close it and turn the page down
> And never come back,

Returned to what we once were before we became what
  we are.
This is the tale the world tells, this is the way it ends.
(*BY* 22)

"Buffalo Yoga" significantly closes on the word "end." Thus the poem itself reflects the finality of death and futility of a world in which "we read" its "magic book" and though we might try to make our mark—"turn the page down"—it is revealed we "never come back." Instead we return to what we were before we came, which the poem implies is nothingness.

"Buffalo Yoga" is followed by three "codas," and in this way the poem in miniature reflects the plan of the trilogy of trilogies: codas followed *The World of the Ten Thousand Things* and *Negative Blue,* and *The Grave of the Right Hand* worked as a prologue to *Country Music.* The first coda of "Buffalo Yoga" is perhaps the strongest and notes,

We'd like the fog to drift and rise, but it hugs the ground.
Like words we meant to say, but didn't.
We'd like to tell the departed to come back,
                    to say we're sorry for what we didn't say.
If, in fact, they're up there.
If, in fact, they're not still here,
                    still hugging the ground like the fog, like us.
(*BY* 27)

As with the ending of the main poem "Buffalo Yoga," there appears little redemption here. The hope that the speaker may be able to speak to the dead once more, to share with them all he was not able to say before, is stifled by the thought that such a meeting will likely never come. The dead have probably gone nowhere, but cling to the ground like the fog, which is related to words in the passage.

Buffalo Yoga picks up on the strategy Wright first used in *The Other Side of the River* in which he populated his poems with individuals; this is evident in such pieces as "Portrait of the Artist in a Prospect of Stone," "Rosso Venexiano," and "Arrivederci Kingsport." In addition to naming important people from the speaker's past, this last poem also introduces a new theme for Wright: the changing of landscape. As the speaker looks back on Kingsport, Tennessee, Wright's hometown, he reflects that the town he knew as a boy no longer resembles its twenty-first-century reality:

It's all Interstate anymore,
                                        the sedge fields Ted Glynn and I
Would shoot doves on. Or underwater.
The Country Music Highway, out of the hollers and
  backwash
Of southeastern Kentucky, old U.S. 23,
Has carried the boys to a different demarcation,
Their voices like field mice in the 21st-century wind.

Goodbye to that stuff,
The late '40s and early '50s and adolescence,
Dolores Urquiza and Clara Hall
                                    —memory's music just out of tune—
Drifting in their 7th-grade frocks across the Civic Auditorium
  floor.
Goodbye to Sundays, and band practice,
                                                    the backseats of cars,
Goodbye to WKPT and everybody's song.

(*BY* 46)

The speaker realizes that with his passing all these memories will be lost:

> Everything going away again and again toward the light.
> Who will remember Christina Marsh and Bobby Step,
> now that I'm gone?
>
> Who will remember the frog famine,
> Now that the nameless roads
> have carried us all from town?
> (*BY* 46)

While the speaker may worry about how his memories will persist, the poem becomes the vessel in which these details of people and their place are saved. The speaker himself is one of the guilty ones in that he, too, let the road carry him from town.

"My Own Little Civil War" carries on the theme of memory and proves one of *Buffalo Yoga*'s most vivid poems. As its title indicates, the poem is concerned with the speaker's southern heritage. Earlier in the book, the Civil War had been evoked in "Buffalo Yoga Coda I" with the "low deck, Montana Sky ~ color of cold Confederate uniforms" (*BY* 25). In "My Own Little Civil War," the speaker begins by announcing, "I come from the only county in Tennessee that did not secede / Throughout the entire Civil War, ~ Sullivan County, / Rock-ribbed, recalcitrant, Appalachian cornerstone" (*BY* 64). He relates how his "great-grandfather Wright" served with Robert E. Lee and "ended up, / Lucky lad, a staff officer in the general's command" (*BY* 64). The speaker then contrasts his great-grandfather to Lee:

> After the war he went back to Lexington, with Lee,
> The general to Washington College and immortality,
> Capt. Wright at the far end of town,
> still marching away the lost cause.

Marse Robert has his horse and white tomb
Under the oak trees.
My great-grandfather has his name in a long thin line
Of others who were Captains of the Corps of Cadets,
too little, boys, too late.
(*BY* 64–65)

The diminished state of the great-grandfather reflects the toll of the war on the general southern population. Wright shares the story of his other "great-grandfather," Penzel, whose tale is told also in "Arkansas Traveller" in *The Other Side of the River,* especially his participation at the Battle of Chickamauga. After sharing some excerpts from period letters from a man identified as Isaac Wright, the speaker concludes the poem:

wrapped in the wax paper,
Among the letters, is another small envelope
Containing a lock, so called,
of Robert E. Lee's hair,
Sent by him to the wife of the lucky lad from VMI . . .
That's it, my own little Civil War—
a lock of hair,
A dozen unreadable letters,
An obit or two,
And half the weight and half-life
of a half-healed and hurting world.
(*BY* 66; Wright's ellipses)

The enduring wounds of the war are evident in the "half-healed and hurting world." In this line the speaker, despite his love for the South, acknowledges the shortcomings of his homeland. The difficulty of resisting the pull of history is evident in the speaker himself who by telling the stories of his Confederate great-grandfathers at least partially glorifies them. Nevertheless the poem teaches that it is only by moving forward that healing can take place.

Near the end of *Buffalo Yoga* appears another poem written about an individual close to the speaker. "Sun-Saddled, Coke-Copping, Bad-Boozing Blues" serves to commemorate a life, "*Tim McIntire (1944–1986)*" (*BY* 69). Like other poems in this book (such as "Portrait of the Artist in a Prospect of Stone") and elsewhere in Wright's corpus, this poem proceeds from its speaker looking at a photograph, remembering the past. The speaker reveals that McIntire was a musician and he had helped him with a song. The speaker then tells how "We all sang in the chorus ~ back in L.A., in the recording studio, / Holly and I and Bill Myers and Kelly and Johnny Rubinstein. / Such joyful music, so long ago, ~ before the coke crash and the whiskey blows (*BY* 68). The poem directly addresses its subject at the end:

> Renaissance Boy,
> With coke up your nose and marijuana in your eye,
> We loved you the best we could, but nobody loved you
> enough.
> Except Miss Whiskey.
> You roll in your sweet baby's arms now, as once you said you
> would.
>
> (*BY* 69)

As with much of *Buffalo Yoga*, there is a frankness here that intertwines with sadness. The speaker, for example, does not gloss over the shortcomings of the individual; his use of illegal drugs is neither deplored nor regretted directly. But there is a tenderness, evident also in the sections of "Buffalo Yoga" on Tom

Andrews, that shows the speaker's connection with his subject: "we loved you the best we could." Wright's next book, *Scar Tissue,* moves away from the largely elegiac mood of *Buffalo Yoga,* but continues its general approach of being written from the point of view of one not always at ease with the world.

Scar Tissue

The sense of finality that pervades *Buffalo Yoga* is made literal in the first few words of *Scar Tissue:* "Sunset in Appalachia" (*ST* 3). The book feels like final advice to a reader from a speaker who has spent his life thinking and observing, as Wright has. It is now twilight in the Appalachian terrain, a landscape that over the course of Wright's career has at times been a paradise and at others reflected the inferno of internal turmoil of the speaker. The themes of *Buffalo Yoga,* and indeed Wright's previous work, are operative here as well, especially his continuing preoccupation with what he terms elsewhere, "language, landscape, and the idea of God" (*QN* 123).

In a review of the book in *Poetry,* Brian Phillips wrote, "Thirty-five years into [Wright's] decorated career, we know what to expect, and one of the pleasures of *Scar Tissue* is its familiarity."[16] Phillips is among the many reviewers who point out that Wright's style, for better or for worse, has changed little since the late 1970s. For some readers this is an attribute, but for others a liability. Joel Brouwer, for example, complained of the inconclusiveness of the poems, that "sometimes it seems like Wright's project is to find ever more convincing ways to tell us he doesn't have anything to tell us."[17]

They are quite reflective poems nevertheless. The book's first piece, "Appalachian Farewell," takes stock of the speaker's life. He notes, "These are the towns our lives abandoned," and asks, "where were we headed for?" (*ST* 3). The poem recalls "Arrivederci Kingsport" from the last volume in its evocation of the town the speaker loved, now lost entirely except in memory. The speaker offers a supplication:

> Goddess of Bad Roads and Inclement Weather, take down
> Our names, remember us in the drip
> And thaw of the wintry mix, remember us when the light
> cools.
>
> Help us never to get above our raising, help us
> To hold hard to what was there,
> Orebank and Reedy Creek, Surgoinsville down the line.
> (*ST* 3)

What the speaker asks for here is significant: not for forgiveness, as in *Buffalo Yoga,* and not for redemption, but rather to be remembered and to remember himself. When he asks the goddess to help him "hold hard to what was there," he seeks comfort in what he learned and found in the past.

The next poem in the collection, "Last Supper," similarly focuses on the end of things, but it is notable that the end is not tinged with darkness as it is in *Buffalo Yoga.* Rather the speaker simply appears somewhat bewildered at where he finds himself: "I seem to have come to the end of something, but don't know what," he reports (*ST* 4). He is not unlike the wanderer in Dante's *Divine Comedy* who begins his poem by stating, "Midway in our life's journey, I went astray / from the straight road and woke to find myself / alone in a dark wood."[18] Wright's figure similarly finds himself in a state of confusion. He takes comfort in the idea that "one knows / There is no end to the other world, ~ no matter where it is" (*ST* 4). While his mortality may be a problem, now that he is reaching the end of his life, he looks forward to that "other world," which, despite his dubiousness of "where it is," believes is eternal.

The speaker also takes more comfort in God in *Scar Tissue* than in previous books by Wright. The speaker admits to being "a God-fearing agnostic" although he says, "Are you there, Lord, I whisper, ~ knowing he's not around" (*ST* 16). In "The Minor Art of Self-Defense," he announces that "landscape was never a subject matter, it was a technique," and he reveals, "Language was always the subject matter, the idea of God / The ghost that over my little world / Hovered, my mouthpiece for meaning" (*ST* 29). God and language are united here as the speaker seeks to find meaning in the combination of the two. He notes later, in the title poem sequence, that "the urge toward form is the urge toward God, ~ perfection of either / Unhinged, unutterable" (*ST* 37). Form has been a persistent concern for Wright as over the years he has varied the lengths of his poem and lines, always seeking to find the idiom that would best allow him to explore his themes. If his quest for form can be seen as a search for God, as he suggests here, then his poems are deeply religious to a degree not immediately obvious on the surface of the poems.

The theme of religious searching continues into "Matins" (the term for morning prayer in various branches of Christianity), which contends,

> If we were the Rapture's child, if we
> Were the Manichaean boy,
> If we were the Bodhisattva baby,
>   today would be a good day
> To let the light in, or send it out.
> We're not, however. We're Nature's nobodies,
>   and we'd do well

To put on the *wu wei* slippers and find a hard spot
To sit on,
        sinking like nothing through the timed tides of ourselves.
(*ST* 56)

The many references here might require some explanation. In his notes Wright describes the principle of wu wei: "'*Wu wei*': In Taoism and Zen Buddhism, unmotivated action; in Chinese, literally, 'nondoing'" (*ST* 73). Manichaeanism is a Middle Eastern religion that teaches dualism, a battle between light and dark. The rapture refers to the belief common among some Protestant denominations that the faithful will be transported to Heaven to be with Jesus. A Bodhisattva in Buddhism is one who helps others seeking nirvana, as the Buddha himself did. In these disparate references the overlapping religious traditions that Wright has written on for years come together. But the significant point is that the speaker is not one of these chosen people ("Rapture's child," "Manichaean boy," or "Bodhisattva baby"), but someone ordinary, one of "nature's nobodies." Instead he must await the "timed tide" of himself when he will expire. Speaking in the form of "we" allows the speaker to include the reader in his thought, and in this way he identifies himself with the common person.

The nature of the self is the subject of other poems in *Scar Tissue*. In "Pilgrim's Progress" the reader witnesses a return of the dog motif from *Country Music*. The speaker notes, "one's a small dog / At night on the front porch, ~ barking into the darkness / At what he can't see, but smells, somehow, and is suspicious of. / Barking, poor thing, and barking, / With no one at home to call him in, ~ with no one to turn the light on" (*ST* 61). Like the poor dog, the speaker often finds himself feeling as if he is barking into the dark, not knowing for sure if something is truly there. The speaker becomes even more self-critical in "Wrong Notes":

> And what does this matter?
> Not much, unless you're one of those,
> As I am, who hears a music in such things, who thinks,
> When the sun goes down, or the stars do,
> That the tune they're doing is his song,
> That the instruments of the given world
> play only for him.
> (*ST* 27–28)

The speaker questions the very enterprise he has embarked on. It is Wright's method to sit and listen to nature for insight, but here he addresses the possible hubris of thinking the "tune" of the world is played for him. In other words, to imagine himself special enough to receive messages from nature, the landscape, and perhaps God elevates the speaker to a position he does not know that he is comfortable with. And there is no reason to think this song "play[s] only for him"—perhaps it would play for anyone who would listen.

The findings of Wright's meditations are not always so bleak in the book, however. In the case of "Morning Occurrence at Xanadu," the speaker realizes his good fortune:

> Someone who knows how little he knows
> Is like the man who comes to a clearing in the forest,
> and sees the light spikes,
> And suddenly senses how happy his life has been.
> (*ST* 25)

Xanadu is the name of Wright's place in Montana, a place where many of his poems have been set. In this poem it is in the limits of his knowledge that the speaker finds comfort. He is released from the burden of knowing or having to figure out all the complexities of the world. After so many poems attempting to do exactly that, Wright recognizes here the value in not knowing, or at least realizing "how little he knows."

Another of Wright's favorite themes, memory, proves pervasive in *Scar Tissue*. In "The Woodpecker Pecks, But the Hole Does Not Appear," the speaker marvels, "It's hard to imagine how unremembered we all become, / How quickly all that we've done / Is unremembered and unforgiven" (*ST* 68). "The Silent Generation III" similarly expresses dismay for the ease with which people can be forgotten. The speaker speaks in the third person plural:

> Not heavy enough to be the hangman's burden,
> our noosed names
> Are scrawled in the dust discursively, line after line.
> Too strange for our contemporaries,
> we'll prove to be
> Not strange enough for posterity.
> (*ST* 64)

The term *silent generation* refers to the generation born between the mid-1920s and the mid-1930s, immediately preceding the "Baby Boomer" generation, which came of age in the 1960s. Since the silent generation (to which Wright, born in 1935, belongs) came of age in the later 1940s or 1950s, they appear more conservative than the baby boomers and are "silent" by comparison. In this poem Wright worries that this group will be overlooked by the future, that they are "not strange enough for posterity." The speaker's immortality in verse is doubted as he supposes his work has not been innovative enough to be remembered beyond his own time.

The speaker's concern with immortality is not a new theme for Wright by this point, but *Scar Tissue* does find Wright discussing new subjects. A car is the topic of "Appalachia Dog"; the speaker's past construction work is the focus in "Get a Job"; his education is remembered in "College Days"; and the rodeo figures in "The Sodbuster's Saloon and Hall of Fame." Nevertheless many of the features of Wright's poetry persist, such as his favorite locations: the South appears in "Get a Job" and "Archaeology"; Montana in "The Woodpecker Pecks, but the Hole Does Not Appear"; and Italy in "A Short History of My Life," "Scar Tissue II," and "Ghost Days."

One poem in *Scar Tissue* even takes its title from another book of Wright's: "China Traces." Here he writes, "Nature contains no negatives. ~ Nothing is lost there, / The word is. Except the word" (*ST* 55). The term *negatives* evokes *Negative Blue,* and the poem ends with familiar imagery: "In the night, the light assembles the stars" (*ST* 55). The light and stars have proved to be enduring symbols for Wright, typically signifying both transcendence sought through nature and also the limits of our knowledge: we cannot see beyond the stars, to heaven, as the "pilgrim" of *China Trace* could not.

The style of *Scar Tissue* follows Wright's practice in later books: a continuation of the dropped line (although used less extensively than previously), generally shorter poems in the style of those in *Negative Blue* (as well as some very short ones more like *Buffalo Yoga*'s appear), and a title poem broken into individual sections.

Some differences, however, are that Wright uses compound words in a way not common before ("wingrush" [*ST* 8], "river-run" [*ST* 9]) and he continues the practice of *A Short History of the Shadow* and *Buffalo Yoga* in his use of odd descriptions or similes. He writes, for example, of "the cocaine smell of the wind" (*ST* 18); "Our tongues like turnip greens, ~ our dreams a rodeo dog's" (*ST* 38); "Morning, like strawberry Kool-Aid" (*ST* 45). These comparisons allow the speaker and the reader to see humanity and nature in new ways and are reminiscent of the sometimes-surreal moments of earlier Wright poems.

Wright has long tried to teach us new ways to view the world, and that impulse continues in *Scar Tissue*'s final poem, "Singing Lesson." The book closes with the speaker instructing the reader about the importance of listening:

> Therefore, when the Great Mouth with its two tongues of
>   water and ash
> Shall say, Suffer the darkness,
> Suffer the darkness to come unto you,
>   suffer its singsong,
> And you will abide,
> Listen to what the words spell, listen and sing the song.
>   (*ST* 69)

Though the lines seem a directive for the reader, they are as much a commandment for the speaker himself, who knows he must "suffer the darkness" and sing its song. If he did otherwise, he would not be honest with what he feels is the truth of existence.

Ultimately the book offers no more resolution than any of the others. But there is not the distraught and mournful tone of *Buffalo Yoga*. Instead *Scar Tissue* ends thoughtfully, with the speaker listening closely to the world and hoping to sing its song in all its darkness and light. This is precisely what Wright has been doing his whole long writing career.

Notes

Chapter 1—Introduction to Charles Wright

1. Critics such as Jeffrey Walker in *Bardic Ethos and the American Epic Poem* (Baton Rouge: Louisiana State University Press, 1989) and Thomas Gardner in *Discovering Ourselves in Whitman: The Contemporary American Long Poem* (Urbana: University of Illinois Press, 1989) have studied Whitman's influence on later American poets who undertake long poetic works.

2. Ernest Suarez, *Southbound* (Columbia: University of Missouri Press, 1999), 56. Wright alternatively describes the structure of *Country Music,* which he applies also to later trilogies, as "Yesterday, Today and Tomorrow / Down There, Here and Up There." Letter to the author, no date, postmarked 14 September 2007.

3. J. D. McClatchy anticipated this problem with his comment at the time of *Appalachia*'s publication: "it may be that when Charles Wright has published three more collections they will be sheaved together and talk will start of The Tetralogy." "Ars Longa," in *High Lonesome: On the Poetry of Charles Wright,* ed. Adam Giannelli, 110 (Oberlin: Oberlin College Press, 2006).

4. Letter to the author, no date, postmarked 14 September 2007.

5. Thomas Di Salvo, "An Interview with Charles Wright," *Writer's Chronicle* 39 (May/Summer 2007), 44.

6. For an extended study of the development of Wright's dropped line poetics, see Brian Henry, "New Scaffolding for New Arrangements: Charles Wright's Low Riders," *Virginia Quarterly Review* 80, no. 2 (2004): 98–112.

7. Calvin Bedient, "Tracing Charles Wright," in *High Lonesome,* 127.

8. See, for example, Ashley Brown, review of *Negative Blue, World Literature Today* 74, no. 4 (2000), 821. See also Edward Hirsch, "From 'The Visionary Poetics of Philip Levine and Charles Wright,'" in *The Point Where All Things Meet: Essays on Charles*

Wright, ed. Tom Andrews, 258 (Oberlin: Oberlin College Press, 1995).

9. Ted Genoways, "An Interview with Charles Wright," *Southern Review* 36 (Spring 2000), 446.

10. Bonnie Costello, "Charles Wright, Giorgio Morandi, and the Metaphysics of the Line," in *High Lonesome,* 304.

11. Wright names Hopkins as one of the two "poets I came to love best." The other is Emily Dickinson. Charles Wright, *Uncollected Prose: Six Guys and a Supplement* (Roanoke College, 2000), 12.

12. Lee Upton, "The Doubting Penitent: Charles Wright's Epiphanies of Abandonment," in *High Lonesome,* 257.

13. Henry Hart, "Charles Wright's *Via Mystica,*" in *High Lonesome,* 325–344.

14. Gerry LaFemina, in a review of *Chickamauga,* analyzed how Wright combines the internal spiritual struggle of the speaker with his external surroundings, concluding: "he reinvents the external landscape by fusing it with the internal landscape and, in so doing, hopes for some redemption." Review of *Chickamauga, Colorado Review* 22, no. 2 (1996), 217.

15. Adam Giannelli, introduction, *High Lonesome,* xii. Early on Wright had considered the alternative title "Tennessee Waltz" for the long work. Suarez, *Southbound,* 54.

16. James Longenbach, "*Appalachia,*" in *High Lonesome,* 97.

Chapter 2—On *Country Music*

1. Richard Tillinghast, "From Michigan and Tennessee," *New York Times Book Review,* 12 December 1982, 14.

2. Jay Parini, "From Scene to Fiery Scene," *Times Literary Supplement,* 1 March 1985, 239.

3. Calvin Bedient, "Slide-Wheeling around the Curves," in *The Point Where All Things Meet: Essays on Charles Wright,* ed. Tom Andrews, 39 (Oberlin: Oberlin College Press, 1995).

4. In a chapter on Wright's work, "Charles Wright: The Remembered Earth," Jay Parini deeply disagrees with Wright's choice of

poems from *The Grave of the Right Hand* for *Country Music.* Parini contends that Wright "mistakenly culled only five mediocre prose poems from his first book, *The Grave of the Right Hand* (1970), killing off a dozen poems of remarkable lyric grace" in the process. *Some Necessary Angels: Essays on Writing and Politics* (New York: Columbia University Press, 1997), 183.

5. Charles Altieri, "Motives in Metaphor: John Ashbery and the Modernist Long Poem," *Genre* 11 (Winter 1978), 653.

6. Ernest Suarez, *Southbound* (Columbia: University of Missouri Press, 1999), 43.

7. John N. Morris, "Making More Sense Than Omaha," *Hudson Review* 27, no. 1 (1974): 107.

8. Sally M. Gall, "Seven from Wesleyan," *Shenandoah* 21, no. 1 (1974): 61.

9. Robert Pinsky, "Description and the Virtuous Use of Words," *Parnassus* 3, no. 2 (1975): 145, 146.

10. Edward Kessler, "The Shortest Distance between Two Poets," *Washington Post Book World,* 5 May 1974, 3.

11. Suarez, *Southbound,* 58.

12. Ibid.

13. Ibid.

14. Michael Chitwood, "Gospel Music: Charles Wright and the High Lonesome," in *High Lonesome: On the Poetry of Charles Wright,* ed. Adam Giannelli, 187 (Oberlin: Oberlin College Press, 2006).

15. Peter Stitt, "Five Reviews," *The Point Where All Things Meet,* 53.

16. John N. Morris, "The Songs Protect Us, in a Way," *Hudson Review* 28, no. 3 (1975): 453.

17. Ibid.

18. Carol Muske, "Ourselves in History," *Parnassus* 4, no. 2 (1976): 120.

19. Helen Vendler, "The Transcendent 'I,'" in *High Lonesome,* 117.

20. Peter Stitt, "Resurrecting the Baroque," in *High Lonesome,* 233.

21. Wright says that Piero della Francesca's painting had the greatest effect on him at first sight of any painting. He notes that he first viewed it in Italy in March 1959, the same place and time at which he read Ezra Pound and was moved to begin his career in poetry. Charles Wright, *Uncollected Prose: Six Guys and a Supplement* (N.p.: Roanoke College, 2000), 7.

22. Joseph Garrison, review of *China Trace, Library Journal* 102 (August 1977): 1654. Jay Parini concurred with Garrison's high estimation of *China Trace:* "Of the first four books, *China Trace* (1977) contains the best work." "From Scene to Fiery Scene," 239.

23. Stitt, "Five Reviews," 55.

24. Richard Jackson, "Worlds Created, Worlds Perceived," *Michigan Quarterly Review* 17, no. 4 (1978): 556. In a particularly hostile review of *China Trace,* David Bromwich argued, "Charles Wright would be more intriguing if he found it not so fine a thing to relax into each inexpensive but portentous phrase as it arose to his his [*sic*] mind and fell from his pen." "I Showed Her My Darkness, She Gave Me a Stone," *Poetry* 133 (December 1978): 169.

25. Michael Chitwood, "Gospel Music: Charles Wright and the High Lonesome," in *High Lonesome,* 187.

26. Suarez, *Southbound,* 43.

27. It is precisely Wright's use of obdurate images such as these that Paul Lake criticizes in an attempt to show the weakness of poets who adopted Deep Imagist strategies. "Return to Metaphor: From Deep Imagist to New Formalist," *New Expansive Poetry: Theory, Criticism, History,* ed. R. S. Gwynn, 134–47 (Ashland, Oreg.: Story Line Press, 1999).

28. Stitt, "Five Reviews," 56.

Chapter 3—On *The World of the Ten Thousand Things*

1. J. D. McClatchy, "Amid the Groves, under the Shadowy Hill, the Generations Are Prepared," *Poetry* 158 (August 1991): 288. Christopher Buckley provided a similarly enthusiastic reading of the

book, calling Wright "a poet of brilliant and original style." "Charles Wright's Hymn," *Poet Lore* 86, no. 3 (1991): 59. Mutlu Konuk Blasing offered another positive review noting, "the collection adds up to more than the sum of its parts," although she worried that sometimes Wright's subjects, specifically his discussion of the plight of the Cherokee in the book's "A Journal of the Year of the Ox," might be misguided. "The American Sublime, c. 1992: What Clothes Does One Wear?," *Michigan Quarterly Review* 31, no. 3 (1992): 436, 441.

2. David Walker, "From '*One for the Rose* and *The Southern Cross*,'" in *High Lonesome: On the Poetry of Charles Wright,* ed. Adam Giannelli, 14 (Oberlin: Oberlin College Press, 2006).

3. J. D. McClatchy, "Ars Longa," in *High Lonesome,* 110. Daniel McGuiness examines the use of the long line in Wright and his contemporary Jorie Graham and decides that in these two poets the long line has gone from being an aesthetic associated with public utterance among such writers as Whitman to a "private long line, a straight shot of interiorality." "The Long Line in Contemporary American Poetry," *Antioch Review* 47 (Summer 1989): 274.

4. Adam Giannelli, introduction, *High Lonesome,* xvi.

5. Peter Stitt, "Five Reviews," *The Point Where All Things Meet: Essays on Charles Wright,* ed. Tom Andrews, 57 (Oberlin: Oberlin College Press, 1995).

6. Richard Tillinghast, "From 'An Elegist's New England, a Buddhist's Dante,'" in *High Lonesome,* 41. David Young, "The Blood Bees of Paradise," in *High Lonesome,* 43. Calvin Bedient, "Tracing Charles Wright," in *High Lonesome,* 134.

7. Walker, "From '*One for the Rose,*'" 10.

8. The editorial notes to this poem in the *Norton Anthology of Contemporary Poetry* point out that the term *cadmium blue* is Wright's invention, based on terms such as *cadmium red.* Jahan Ramazani, Richard Ellmann, and Robert O'Clair, eds., *The Norton Anthology of Modern and Contemporary Poetry,* vol. 2 (New York: W. W. Norton, 2003), 645.

9. James McCorkle, "'Things That Lock Our Wrists to the Past': Self-Portraiture and Autobiography in Charles Wright's Poetry," in *High Lonesome,* 157.

10. J. D. McClatchy, "Under the Sign of the Cross," in *High Lonesome,* 151.

11. Ibid.

12. Mark Jarman, "From 'The Trace of a Story Line,'" in *High Lonesome,* 18. Sidney Burris also made note of Wright's new direction, although Burris focused more on Wright's success in writing poetic sequences as compared to his contemporaries'. "Gaiety, Magic, and War: Ariel and Prospero among Three American Poets," *Kenyon Review* 6 (Summer 1984): 130. Elizabeth Frank praised the new approach of the book, calling attention to its "hard, direct statement and fearlessly drawn conclusions." "The Middle of the Journey," *Nation,* 7 April 1984, 421.

13. Vendler, for example, offers one of the earliest scholarly studies on Wright with a chapter on him in her book *Part of Nature, Part of Us: Modern American Poets* (Cambridge: Harvard University Press, 1980). Vendler has also written many reviews on Wright's books over the years.

14. David Kalstone, "From 'Lives in a Rearview Mirror,'" in *High Lonesome,* 16.

15. Mark Jarman, "From 'The Pragmatic Imagination and the Secret of Poetry,'" in *High Lonesome,* 28. Helen Vendler similarly found strength in the book and wrote, "In his zones of dislocation . . . Wright finds a scene of writing unique to himself and to his historical moment, and phrases it over and over in his musical and grieving half-lines." "Travels in Time," in *High Lonesome,* 35.

16. William Logan, "Season to Season, Day to Day," *New York Times Book Review,* 4 September 1988, 9.

17. Ibid.

18. Walt Whitman, *Leaves of Grass* (New York: Vintage Books, 1992), 247.

19. Ernest Suarez, *Southbound* (Columbia: University of Missouri Press, 1999), 46.

20. Christopher Buckley, "Charles Wright's Hymn," *The Point Where All Things Meet,* 205.

21. McClatchy, "Amid the Groves," 287.

22. Christopher Buckley writes that "Language Journal" is "a wonderfully subtle poem against the tenets of language poetry and deconstruction." "Charles Wright's Hymn," 209.

23. Letter to the author, no date, postmarked 14 September 2007.

Chapter 4—On *Negative Blue*

1. Ernest Suarez, *Southbound* (Columbia: University of Missouri Press, 1999), 56.

2. Daniel Cross Turner, "Oblivion's Glow: The (Post) Southern Sides of Charles Wright: An Interview," *storySouth* (Summer 2005), http://www.storysouth.com/summer2005/wright_interview.html (accessed 15 June 2007). It is noteworthy too that *Negative Blue* also carries four syllables.

3. Ashley Brown, review of *Negative Blue, World Literature Today* 74, no. 4 (2000): 821, 822.

4. Ron Smith, "Charles Wright Excels Once More in New Collection of Verse," *Richmond Times-Dispatch,* 12 November 2000, F4. M. L. Schuldt, "Search Light: Charles Wright Scans the Landscape of Language," *Tucson Weekly,* 16 November 2000, 35.

5. Christina Pugh, review of *Negative Blue, Harvard Review* 21 (2001): 177.

6. Ron Smith, "An Enchanted, Diminished World," in *High Lonesome: On the Poetry of Charles Wright,* ed. Adam Giannelli, 112 (Oberlin: Oberlin College Press, 2006).

7. J. D. McClatchy, "Ars Longa," in *High Lonesome,* 106.

8. Henry Hart, "Charles Wright's *Via Mystica,*" in *High Lonesome,* 329.

9. Two other important studies of mysticism and transcendence in Wright's poetry are Bonnie Costello, "Charles Wright's *Via Negativa:* Landscape, Language, and the Idea of God," *Contemporary Literature* 42 (Summer 2001): 325–46, and Kevin Hart, "La poesia è scala

a Dio: On Reading Charles Wright," *Religion and the Arts* 8, no. 2 (2004): 174–99.

10. Helen Vendler, "The Nothing That Is," in *High Lonesome*, 68. Although Calvin Bedient, in a review of *Chickmauga*, praised Wright as "one of the supreme poets of the physical world," he also criticized Wright's general approach: "Wright keeps trying to graft Zen wisdom onto the quaking aspen of his sensibility." "Poetry and Silence at the End of the Century," *Salmagundi* 111 (Summer 1996): http://proquest.umi.com (journal located in online database *ProQuest*, accessed 7 January 2008). An anonymous reviewer offered high praise for the book: "With *The World of the Ten Thousand Things* (1990), Charles Wright established himself as the premier poet in America. *Chickamauga* confirms this fact." The reviewer also argued *Chickamauga* is a book "to which poets will go for instruction and readers for sustenance." Review of *Chickamauga, Virginia Quarterly* 71 (Autumn 1995): 137.

11. Turner, "Oblivion's Glow."

12. Ibid.

13. James M. Robinson, ed., *The Nag Hammadi Library*, revised edition (New York: HarperCollins, 1988), 135.

14. Ibid., 126.

15. James Longenbach, "From 'Earned Weight,'" in *High Lonesome*, 82.

16. John Berryman, *The Dream Songs* (New York: Noonday, 1996), 376.

17. About the poems in *Black Zodiac*, Carol Muske said they "imply the ultimate impossibility of a story yet somehow deliver, whole and integrated, a psyche, a poet's soul." Quoted in Mel Gussow, "A Good Ear for the Music in His Own Life," *New York Times*, 16 April 1998, late edition, E1, see http://proquest.umi.com (article located in online database *ProQuest*, accessed 7 January 2008). Jacqueline Marcus defended Wright's use of abstractions and heralded *Black Zodiac* as "both elegant and elegiac." "The Imperishable Quiet at the Heart of Form: Charles Wright's *Black Zodiac*," *Literary Review* 41 (Summer 1998): 563, 566. David Wojahn

offered praise for the book and noted that, with *Chickamauga* and extending into *Black Zodiac,* Wright "seemed to have entered a new and far more compelling phase of his career." "Survivalist Selves," *Kenyon Review* 20, nos. 3/4 (1998): 181.

18. Calvin Bedient, "Slide-Wheeling around the Curves," *The Point Where All Things Meet: Essays on Charles Wright,* ed. Tom Andrews, 39 (Oberlin: Oberlin College Press, 1995).

19. Ezra Pound, *Personae: The Shorter Poems,* eds. Lea Beachler and A. Walton Litz, 185 (New York: New Directions, 1990).

20. Willard Spiegelman, "Landscape and Identity: Charles Wright's Backyard Metaphysics," *Southern Review* 40 (Winter 2004): 172–96.

21. James Longenbach, "*Appalachia,*" in *High Lonesome,* 95.

22. Turner, "Oblivion's Glow," http://www.storysouth.com/summer2005/wright_interview.html (accessed 15 June 2007).

23. Adam Kirsch, "Between Heaven and Earth," in *High Lonesome,* 99.

24. Ibid.

25. Ibid., 100.

26. McClatchy, "Ars Longa," 105.

27. Adam Giannelli, introduction, *High Lonesome,* xii. Longenbach, "*Appalachia,*" 97.

28. Thomas Di Salvo, "An Interview with Charles Wright," *Writer's Chronicle* 39 (May/Summer 2007), 44.

29. William Butler Yeats, *The Yeats Reader: A Portable Compendium of Poetry, Drama, and Prose,* revised edition, ed. Richard J. Finneran, 103 (New York: Scribner, 2002).

30. Ibid., 105.

31. Suarez, *Southbound,* 56.

Chapter 5—On Later Books

1. James Longenbach, "*Appalachia,*" in *High Lonesome: On the Poetry of Charles Wright,* ed. Adam Giannelli, 97 (Oberlin: Oberlin College Press, 2006).

2. Thomas Di Salvo, "An Interview with Charles Wright," *Writer's Chronicle* 39 (May/Summer 2007): 44.

3. Letter to the author, no date, postmarked 14 September 2007.

4. Jay Parini, "A 'Thirst for the Divine,'" *Nation,* 20 May 2002, 30.

5. Michael Scharf, review of *A Short History of the Shadow, Publishers Weekly* 25 (February 2002): 56.

6. Lee Oser, review of *A Short History of the Shadow, World Literature Today* 77 (April/June 2003): 106. Oser's concern was echoed by William Logan, who wrote, "Too many of these poems sink into the portentous tone that passes for wisdom in contemporary poetry." "Falls the Shadow," *New Criterion* 20, no. 10 (2002): 75. Ron Smith worried that "some of these new poems are probably more abstract than they need to be." "Wright Continues Lyrical Trips in Nature," *Richmond Times-Dispatch,* 29 September 2002, F4.

7. Thomas Gardner, *A Door Ajar: Contemporary Writers and Emily Dickinson* (New York: Oxford University Press, 2006), 108.

8. "Night Rider" is the subject of Willard Spiegelman, interview, *Literary Imagination* 2 (Winter 2000): 108–21.

9. An exception to this is Ron Smith in "Charles Wright Excels Once More in New Collection of Verse," *Richmond Times-Dispatch,* 12 November 2000, F4.

10. The Book of Common Prayer (N.p.: Seabury Press, 1979), 358.

11. Michael Scharf, review of *Buffalo Yoga, Publishers Weekly,* 26 April 2004, 56.

12. Richard Rand, Review of *Buffalo Yoga, Harvard Review,* 27 (2004): 203. Gerry LaFemina published a similarly positive review, noting the strength of Wright's musical language. "'Like Intercessionary Prayers to Purgatory'—Charles Wright's *Buffalo Yoga,*" *Journal* 28 (Autumn 2004): 101–5.

13. Ezra Pound, *The Cantos* (New York: New Directions, 1995), 822.

14. T. S. Eliot, *The Complete Poems and Plays: 1909–1950* (New York: Harcourt Brace, 1952), 7.

15. Wright describes the poem as being a "valedictory" to Andrews in Di Salvo, "An Interview with Charles Wright," 44.

16. Brian Phillips, "Eight Takes," *Poetry* 189 (December 2006): 235.

17. Joel Brouwer, "A World in Permanent Flux," *New York Times Book Review,* 17 September 2006, 26.

18. Dante, *The Divine Comedy,* trans. John Ciardi (New York: New American Library, 2003), 16.

Selected Bibliography

Primary Sources

Chapbooks

The Voyage. Iowa City: Patrician Press, 1963.
Six Poems. London: Royal College of Art, 1965.
The Dream Animal. Toronto: Anansi, 1968.
Private Madrigals. Madison, Wis.: Abraxas Press, 1969.
The Venice Notebook. Boston: Barn Dream Press, 1971.
Backwater. Santa Ana, Calif.: Golem Press, 1973.
Colophons. Iowa City: Windhover Press, 1977.
Wright: A Profile. Iowa City: Grilled Flowers Press, 1979.
Dead Color. Salem, Oreg.: Charles Seluzicki, 1980.
Four Poems of Departure. Portland, Oreg.: Trace Editions, 1983.
Yard Journal. Richmond, Va.: Laurel Press, 1985.
Five Journals. New York: Red Ozier Press, 1986.
A Journal of the Year of the Ox: A Poem. Iowa City: Windhover Press, 1988.
Xionia: Poems. Iowa City: Windhover Press, 1990.
North American Bear. Winona, Minn.: Sutton Hoo Press, 1999.
Night Music. Exeter, UK: Stride, 2001.
The Wrong End of the Rainbow. Louisville, Ky.: Sarabande, 2005.

Collections and Collected Volumes

The Grave of the Right Hand. Middletown, Conn.: Wesleyan University Press, 1970.
Hard Freight. Middletown, Conn.: Wesleyan University Press, 1973.
Bloodlines. Middletown, Conn.: Wesleyan University Press, 1975.
China Trace. Middletown, Conn.: Wesleyan University Press, 1977.
The Southern Cross. New York: Random House, 1981.
Country Music: Selected Early Poems. Middletown, Conn.: Wesleyan University Press, 1982.

The Other Side of the River. New York: Random House, 1984.

Zone Journals. New York: Farrar, Straus & Giroux, 1988; Exeter, U.K.: Stride, 1997.

The World of the Ten Thousand Things: Poems 1980–1990. New York: Farrar, Straus & Giroux, 1990.

Chickamauga. New York: Farrar, Straus & Giroux, 1995.

Black Zodiac. New York: Farrar, Straus & Giroux, 1997.

Appalachia. New York: Farrar, Straus & Giroux, 1998.

Negative Blue: Selected Later Poems. New York: Farrar, Straus & Giroux, 2000; Exeter, U.K.: Stride, 2000.

A Short History of the Shadow. New York: Farrar, Straus & Giroux, 2002.

Buffalo Yoga. New York: Farrar, Straus & Giroux, 2004.

Snake Eyes. Exeter, U.K.: Stride, 2004. British edition of *A Short History of the Shadow* and *Buffalo Yoga.*

Scar Tissue. New York: Farrar, Straus & Giroux, 2006.

Translations by Wright

Campana, Dino. *Orphic Songs.* Oberlin, Ohio: Oberlin College Press, 1984.

Montale, Eugenio. *The Storm and Other Poems.* Oberlin, Ohio: Oberlin College Press,
1978.

———. *Motets.* Iowa City: Windhover Press, 1981.

———. *Selected Poems.* Trans. Jonathan Galassi, Charles Wright, and David Young. Oberlin, Ohio: Oberlin College Press, 2004.

Interviews/Nonfiction

Halflife: Improvisations and Interviews, 1977–1987. Ann Arbor: University of Michigan Press, 1988.

Quarter Notes: Improvisations and Interviews. Ann Arbor: University of Michigan Press, 1995.

Uncollected Prose: Six Guys and a Supplement. N.p.: Roanoke College, 2000.

Secondary Sources

Books

Andrews, Tom, ed. *The Point Where All Things Meet: Essays on Charles Wright.* Oberlin, Ohio: Oberlin College Press, 1995. A collection of early reviews and essays on Wright. Revised by Adam Giannelli as *High Lonesome: On the Poetry of Charles Wright.*

Denham, Robert D. *Charles Wright: A Companion to the Late Poetry, 1988–2007.* Jefferson, N.C.: McFarland Publishing, 2008. In addition to a useful bibliography, provides invaluable glosses and commentaries on Wright's poems collected in *Negative Blue* and in subsequent books.

Giannelli, Adam, ed. *High Lonesome: On the Poetry of Charles Wright.* Oberlin, Ohio: Oberlin College Press, 2006. An essential resource for readers of Wright's poetry. Includes reviews of Wright's books and important articles by such critics as Henry Hart, Bonnie Costello, and Lee Upton. Includes an extensive bibliography.

Book Chapters

Because of the ease with which the reader may find essays on Wright in *The Point Where All Things Meet* and *High Lonesome* and important interviews with him in *Halflife* and *Quarter Notes,* the list that follows is restricted to items not represented in those volumes.

Daniels, Kate. "Porch-Sitting and Southern Poetry." In *The Future of Southern Letters,* edited by Jefferson Humphries and John Lowes, 61–71. New York: Oxford University Press, 1996. Looks at issues in Southern writing, particularly storytelling and the changing social conditions in the South, and ends by reading Wright's poem "The Southern Cross" as exemplary of the strength of Southern poetry.

Davis, V. William. "Making the World with Words: A Reading of Charles Wright's 'Appalachian Book of the Dead.'" In *Latitude*

63° North: Proceedings of the 8th International Region and Nation Literature Conference, Östersund, Sweden 2–6 August 2000, edited by David Bell, 255–70. Östersund, Sweden: Mid-Sweden University College, 2002. Argues that in Wright's work language and landscape merge, especially in his sequence "The Appalachian Book of the Dead."

Gardner, Thomas. *A Door Ajar: Contemporary Writers and Emily Dickinson.* New York: Oxford University Press, 2006, 70–94. Among his discussions on the work of writers such as Susan Howe and Jorie Graham, Gardner also includes "Restructured and Restrung: Charles Wright's *Zone Journals,*" a chapter on Wright's *Zone Journals* and its connections to the Dickinsonian tradition in American verse.

Lake, Paul. "Return to Metaphor: From Deep Imagist to New Formalist." In *New Expansive Poetry: Theory, Criticism, History,* edited by R. S. Gwynn, 134–147. Ashland, Oreg.: Story Line Press, 1999. Looks at Wright's "At Zero" from *China Trace* to point out the obdurate and abstract nature of some poets who adopted "Deep Imagist" practices.

Parini, Jay. "Charles Wright: The Remembered Earth." In *Some Necessary Angels: Essays on Writing and Politics,* 181–200. New York: Columbia University Press, 1997. Offers an overview of Wright's work up through *Zone Journals;* promotes certain poems from *The Grave of the Right Hand* that Wright did not keep for *Country Music;* and emphasizes the religious nature of the poet.

Journal Articles

"Charles Wright Issue." *Iron Mountain Review* 8 (Spring 1992). Published on occasion of the Charles Wright Literary Festival held at Emory and Henry College in Virginia, 10–11 October 1991. Includes materials that were all later reprinted elsewhere: an interview and nonfiction by Wright published in *Quarter Notes* and essays published in *The Point Where All Things Meet* and then in

High Lonesome. Contains a bibliography of work by and on Wright up to that point.

Collins, Floyd. "Metamorphosis within the Poetry of Charles Wright." *Gettysburg Review* 4 (Summer 1991): 464–479. An extended review-essay focusing primarily on *The World of the Ten Thousand Things.* Traces the development of Wright's style and content up to *Xionia.*

Costello, Bonnie. "Charles Wright's *Via Negativa:* Landscape, Language, and the Idea of God." *Contemporary Literature* 42 (Summer 2001): 325–46. Studies the visionary nature of Wright's poetry over his career, but especially in *Negative Blue.* Points out that Wright is working against Romantic ideals of mysticism.

Garrison, David. "'An Old Song Handles My Heart': Charles Wright and the Sweet Failure of Music." *Kentucky Philological Review* 6 (1991): 9–14. Attempts to address the issue of Wright's aloofness and the critics who assert that poetry should directly address societal concerns. Argues that Wright's attention to language shows him as engaged with his culture as one could hope from a poet.

———. "From Feeling to Form: Image as Translation in the Poetry of Charles Wright." *The Midwest Quarterly* 41, no. 1 (1999): 33–47. Focuses on Wright's use of imagery as a way to communicate the poet's experience of the world and universal human feelings.

Hahn, Robert. "The Mockingbird's Chops: Charles Wright in Italian." *Parnassus: Poetry in Review* 29, nos. 1–2 (2005): 349–369. Argues the difficulty of translating Wright's work into Italian because of his distinctive poetic tone.

Hammer, Langdon. "The Latches of Paradise: Charles Wright's Meditations and Memories at Year's End." *American Scholar* 74 (Autumn 2005): 73–74. A very brief reading of Wright's "Appalachian Autumn" is presented.

Hart, Kevin. "La poesia è scala a Dio: On Reading Charles Wright." *Religion and the Arts* 8, no. 2 (2004): 174–199. Offers a well-detailed perspective on the issue of transcendence in literary studies overall and in Wright's poetry in particular.

Henry, Brian. "New Scaffolding for New Arrangements: Charles Wright's Low Riders." *Virginia Quarterly Review* 80 (Spring 2004): 98–112. Examines the development of Wright's dropped line approach, especially in later work such as *Buffalo Yoga*.

———. "Southern Cross: The Inheritance of Charles Wright." *Quarterly West* 46 (1998): 196–202. Presents a brief overview of Wright's career and themes, especially his preoccupation with the South, religion, and landscape.

Hix, H. L. "Charles Wright and a Case of Foreshortened Influence." *Notes on Contemporary Literature* 18 (January 1988): 4–6. Suggests that two poems from Wright's *China Trace* are closely patterned on poems by W. S. Merwin and thus Wright suffers from not looking far enough into the past for poetic inspiration.

Longenbach, James. "Disjunction in Poetry." *Raritan* 20 (Spring 2001): 20–36. Describes different types of disjunction in verse, using diverse examples, and reads a poem from Wright's *Appalachia* in its concluding paragraphs.

McGuiness, Daniel. "The Long Line in Contemporary American Poetry." *Antioch Review* 47 (Summer 1989): 269–86. Examines the use of long poetic line in the tradition of American verse and specifically in the work of Charles Wright and Jorie Graham. Suggests that Wright and Graham use the once-public long line for more personal purposes.

Spiegelman, Willard. "Landscape and Identity: Charles Wright's Backyard Metaphysics." *Southern Review* 40 (Winter 2004): 172–96. Reprinted in Spiegelman's *How Poets See the World: The Art of Description in Contemporary Poetry*, 82–111. New York: Oxford University Press, 2005. Offers an overview of Wright's poetry, addressing a number of issues related to the poet's verse such as landscape, art, and poetic technique.

Walton, Anthony. "The Journey Within." *Oxford American* 37 (January/February 2001): 67–73. A nonscholarly profile of Wright's writing around the time of the publication of *Negative Blue*.

Wright, Stuart. "Charles Wright: A Bibliographic Chronicle, 1963–1985." *Bulletin of Bibliography* 43, no. 1 (1986): 3–12. An indispensable bibliography of Wright's writing career up to 1985, showing first publication of individual poems.

Zawacki, Andrew. "Reading Wright in the Wrong Country." *Thumbscrew* 8 (Summer 1997): 74–78. Argues that Wright's work is unjustly ignored in England, despite the universality of his spiritual searching, and calls for a change in this situation.

Interviews

Bourgeois, Louis. "An Interview with Charles Wright." *Carolina Quarterly* 56, nos. 2–3 (2004): 30–37. Focuses on the southern literary tradition and Wright's place in it; also discusses the importance of prosody and the nature of the prose poem.

Di Salvo, Thomas. "An Interview with Charles Wright." *Writer's Chronicle* 39 (May/Summer 2007): 40–45. Shows Wright reflecting on his three books that followed *Negative Blue* (*A Short History of the Shadow, Buffalo Yoga,* and *Scar Tissue*) and their relationship to earlier work, along with favorite subjects of Wright's such as spirituality and poetics.

Gardner, Thomas. Interview. *A Door Ajar: Contemporary Writers and Emily Dickinson.* New York: Oxford University Press, 2006, 95–108. As the title implies, considers Wright's connection to Dickinson, who Wright has continually cited as an important influence.

Genoways, Ted. "An Interview with Charles Wright." *Southern Review* 36 (Spring 2000): 442–52. Wright reflects on his poetics, especially his method of syllable counting, as well as recalls his time at the University of Iowa and shares his thoughts after completing *Appalachia.*

Schuldt, Morgan. "An Interview with Charles Wright." *Sonora Review* 43 http://www.coh.arizona.edu/sonora/43/interview.html (accessed 10 May 2007). Includes Wright's reflections on influences such as Ezra Pound, his reading of the Language Poets, and his then-new book, *A Short History of the Shadow.*

Suarez, Ernest. *Southbound.* Columbia: University of Missouri Press, 1999, 39–61. Provides an important interview with Wright, conducted at the time he was completing *Negative Blue,* and including his thoughts on ending his trilogy of trilogies. Also presents a bibliography on Wright.

Spiegelman, Willard. Interview. *Literary Imagination* 2 (Winter 2000): 108–21. Focuses on Wright's poem "Night Rider" but also includes reflections on his writing process, as well as on works such as "Homage to Paul Cézanne," and Wright's relationship to past poets such as Pound, Stevens, and Yeats.

Turner, Daniel Cross. "Oblivion's Glow: The (Post) Southern Sides of Charles Wright: An Interview." *storySouth* (Summer 2005): http://www.storysouth.com/summer2005/wright_interview.html (accessed 15 June 2007). Considers Wright's southern ties as well as the influence of cinema on his work.

Vadnie, Rebecca Swain. "Interview with Poet Charles Wright." *Orlando Sentinel,* 16 October 2002: *EbscoHost* 14 May 2007. http://web.ebscohost.com (accessed 14 May 2007). A relatively short interview, focusing especially on *A Short History of the Shadow.*

Index